EXPLOITABLE VULNERABILITIES OF IRAN'S ISLAMIC REVOLUTIONARY GUARD CORPS

Within the framework commonly referred to as the instruments of national power, states wield their influence both domestically and externally through various diplomatic, informational, military, and economic tools. The elected and appointed leadership of the Islamic Republic of Iran has empowered the nation's Islamic Revolutionary Guard Corps (IRGC), or *Pasdaran*, to employ these tools in such scope and scale that the IRGC has become the center of gravity for the security of the regime, as well as for its economy, domestic and foreign policies, and influence over its society. This empowerment, enabled by a lack of credible state checks and balances or separation of powers, is a critical strength for the *Pasdaran* and the current regime. However, within each of the instruments of national power, the IRGC has a number of exploitable vulnerabilities. While portrayed and self-promoted domestically as ideologically pure guardians of the revolution and defenders of Islam, the IRGC is neither omnipotent nor omnipresent. Rather, the *Pasdaran* and its vast network of alumni and advocates are subject to factionalism, internal strife, and exposure of its incompetence. This research paper will describe how the IRGC implements each of the Islamic Republic of Iran's instruments of national power, assess the vulnerabilities resulting from the implementation of these tools, and offer options for exploiting these vulnerabilities.

1

The Islamic Revolution Guards Corps, organized in the early days of the triumph of the Revolution, is to be maintained so that it may continue in its role of guarding the Revolution and its achievements. The scope of the duties of this Corps, and its areas of responsibility, in relation to the duties and areas of responsibility of the other armed forces, are to be determined by law, with emphasis on brotherly cooperation and harmony among them.[1]

The *Pasdaran* derives its legal authority from Article 150 of the Islamic

Republic of Iran's constitution. In accordance with Ayatollah Khomeini's intent,

Iran's Revolutionary Council tasked the IRGC in eight broad categories:

1) Apprehending or liquidating counter-revolutionary elements
2) Battling armed counterrevolutionaries
3) Defending against attacks and the activities of foreign forces inside Iran
4) Coordinating and cooperating with the country's armed forces
5) Training subordinate IRGC personnel in moral, ideological, and politico-military matters
6) Assisting the Islamic Republic in the implementation of the Islamic Revolution 7) Supporting liberation movements and their call for justice of the oppressed people of the world under the tutelage of the leader of the Revolution of the Islamic Republic
8) Utilizing the human resources and expertise of the IRGC to deal with national calamities and unexpected catastrophes and supporting the developmental plans of the Islamic Republic to completely maximize the IRGC's resources [2]

In light of the fact that Supreme Leader Ayatollah Khomeini established

the *Pasdaran* as an internal security service dedicated to the preservation of the

Islamic Revolution, it is useful to examine the IRGC's role within the military

instrument of national power before addressing its less traditional activities in the

diplomatic, information, and economic instruments. As Khomeini consolidated

power after deposing Shah Mohammad Reza Pahlavi, he balanced the counter-

revolutionary threat he perceived from Iran's conventional military with the IRGC,

a trusted parallel military structure specifically beholden to him and his revolutionary principles. In order to maintain internal order and suppress dissent, Khomeini also formalized the multiple post-revolution militias by forming the *Basij* (Mobilization of the Oppressed). Even though the IRGC is constitutionally directed to coordinate with Iran's conventional military forces and is nominally subordinate to a joint headquarters that overseas the security services and Law Enforcement Forces (LEF), the *Pasdaran* answers directly only to Ali al Khamenei, the republic's Supreme Leader. This direct access to the Supreme Leader and his consistent and considerable support for the IRGC makes the *Pasdaran* peerless among military, intelligence, law enforcement, intelligence, and security services in Iran. It is not coincidental that Iran's Minister of Defense, Ahmad Vahidi, is a former IRGC *Qods* (Jerusalem) Force commander, He is also the subject of an Interpol Red Notice for his role in the 1994 attacks on Israeli and Jewish facilities in Buenes Aires, his recruitment of Saudi *Hezballah* terrorists responsible for the 1996 Khobar Tower attack, and his involvement in the assassinations of Iranian dissidents in Europe in the late 1990s.[3] The placement and access of current and former *Pasdaran* and *Basij* commanders and officers throughout Iran's military, law enforcement, and internal security services mitigates intra-agency resistance to the *Padaran's* independence and direct access to the Commander in Chief, Supreme Leader Khamenei. (Ref Table 1, IRGC Personnel and Alumni in Key Positions)

The *Artesh*, Iran's conventional military ground force, consists of approximately 220,000 troops, as compared to the IRGC's 125,000. The *Artesh* is more heavily armed with the equipment and technology currently available to them after decades of sanctions. However, the *Pasdaran* maintains primacy over and responsibility for Iran's most critical national security initiatives to include cyber warfare, Iran's intermediate range ballistic missile program, and naval responsibility for the Arabian Gulf and the Strait of Hormuz. This is in addition to its expansive and growing role in domestic security. There is also widespread assessment that the IRGC is intimately involved in Iran's nuclear program. As the entity responsible for Iran's ballistic missile program, as well as its asymmetric warfare capabilities, the *Pasdaran* has the means to deliver critical or sub-critical fissile material payloads by traditional or unconventional means. The IRGC's responsibility for military and technological research and testing also suggests a logical involvement in any potential current or future nuclear weapons development. It is unlikely a coincidence that the IRGC's research center's website published and article titled, "The Day after Iran's First Nuclear Test Is a Normal Day" a few days before President Ahmadinejad stated, "[if Iran] want[s] to make a bomb, we are not afraid of anyone...and no one can do a damn thing."[4] Major General Mohsen Rezai, Secretary General of the Expediency Council and former Commander of the IRGC said in March 2006, "If we master nuclear technology, we will be transformed into a regional superpower and will dominate 17 Muslim countries in this neighborhood."[5]

Since October 2007, the IRGC also formally controls the *Basij*, a geographically based reserve force of 90,000 which can mobilize up to 1,000,000 personnel. Since the 1994 riots, the *Basij* has assumed a larger role in internal security, receiving training in riot control in order to quell student or opposition uprisings.[6] The *Basij* also provides the IRGC a network of eyes and ears across Iran, maintaining a presence in all major universities.

In September 2007, Supreme Leader Khamenei replaced IRGC Commander Major General Yahya Rahim Safavi, with Major General Mohammad Ali Jafari, formerly commander of the IRGC's Strategic Studies Center. Jafari had long held that the greatest security threat to the regime was an internal "Velvet Revolution" supported by external actors rather than a conventional invasion of Iran by another state or a collection of states.[7] Jafari was instrumental in formally subordinating the *Basij* to the IRGC, stating that the IRGC was, "a military-political-cultural organization sharing the same organizational goals as the *Basij*" and that "half of the Revolutionary Guards' mission is placed on the shoulders of the *Basij*."[8] Jafari also implemented his Mosaic Doctrine for the defense of Iran, restructuring the IRGC and *Basij* into 31 commands, one per province and two for Tehran. The purpose of decentralizing command and control was to improve IRGC Commanders' ability to recruit locally, extend the IRGC's and Supreme Leader's network of eyes and ears across every province, secure the IRGC and *Basij's* role in quelling riots, and disperse IRGC command and control in the event of an external attack.[9]

The IRGC's military doctrine also emphasizes asymmetric or irregular warfare as a means to mitigate the technological capability and capacity gap in it perceives in a scenario of conventional conflict on Iranian soil with another state or states. In August 2005, when he was the commander of the IRGC Center for Strategy, Major General Jafari stated, "As the enemy is far more advanced technologically than we are, we have been using what is called asymmetric warfare methods... Our forces are now well prepared for it."[10] The driving principle is to defeat the stronger adversary's will to continue to fight rather than defeat the enemy's military forces in conventional terms. The tenets of this doctrine include, but are not limited to the following: decentralized command and control of dispersed forces to mitigate an enemy's superior air power and dominance of the electro-magnetic spectrum, incorporation of unconventional tactics and terrorism in response options, concentration of capabilities against an enemy's strategic weak points which are not necessarily military in nature, offensive retaliatory strikes against the enemy outside the war zone, targeting of the enemy's national popular support through information warfare, and emphasis on the power of religious zeal and martyrdom.[11],[1] In May 2004, Hassan Abbasi, the Director of the Center for Doctrinal Studies at the IRGC's Imam Hussain University bluntly summarized the IRGC's intent to employ terrorist tactics,

> "The Islamic world needs suicide bombers... I am a theoretician of terror and violence... We are proud of terrorism, which makes the foundations of unbelief tremble... We have identified the US' Achilles heel and have coordinated with terrorist organizations... We caused the US economic growth to drop and we will cause its disintegration"[12]

Hassan Abbasi and Major General Jafari were the key architects of Iran's doctrine of asymmetric warfare. Jafari's ascendance to command the IRGC and his consolidation of power and political influence since 2009 demonstrate the Supreme Leader's support for this doctrine and its proactive employment.

---

[1] The concept of martyrdom for the sake of Islam as a religious duty is an integral part of the IRGC indoctrination program, with its roots in Shia theology and Iranian culture. Military success depends more on the human factor and adherence to the Iranian revolutionary brand of Islamic faith and ideology than technology, training, and skills of the soldiers.

In order to effectively employ this doctrine, the IRGC must maintain its influence over the population through non-military means and non-military instruments of national power. The IRGC must also maintain a capability to take the conflict outside its borders through unconventional tactics and asymmetric warfare. The *Pasdaran's Qods* (Jerusalem) Force is its primary tool in that endeavor. The Jerusalem Force will be addressed separately in subsequent discussion of the IRGC's influence outside the borders of Iran.

For all of its influence in the military instrument of national power, the IRGC and its asymmetric warfare doctrine have multiple vulnerabilities. The IRGC's blatant disregard for constitutionally mandated command and control structures, its independence from the Ministry of Defense, and its liberal interpretation of its authority put the *Pasdaran* on shaky legal ground. Iranian liberals and oppositionist make a strong argument that the IRGC has exceeded its authority to the point of acting as an extralegal paramilitary element operating above the law. Mohsen Sazegara, one of the IRGC's founding members and now a political dissident, described the *Pasdaran*, "I don't know of any other organization in any country like the Revolutionary Guards. It's something like the Communist Party, the KGB, a business complex, and the mafia.[13]

The duality of the parallel military structures between the IRGC and *Artesh* creates inefficiencies, violates unity of command, and promotes factionalism. The *Pasdaran's* ascendance has come at the expense of both the *Artesh* and the domestic Law Enforcement Forces in terms of resources, authority, and political capital. The resulting friction among the security services has resulted in poor coordination, a lack of integration, and un-sustainability.[14] The IRGC has long promoted itself as the Republic's savior, based on its performance in the Iran-Iraq war. This implies that the *Artesh* and the Iranian Navy failed the Republic, necessitating the IRGC's and *Basij's* heroic sacrifices and martyrdom in order to preserve the revolution. An alternative viewpoint is that the IRGC inserted itself into the forefront of that war in order to secure its enduring prominence after the conflict. Additionally, military analysts both inside and outside of Iran contend that the IRGC's costly human wave tactics unnecessarily prolonged the conflict at an exorbitant cost in terms of blood and treasure.[15] The *Pasdaran's* revisionist historical portrayal of its role in the Iran-Iraq war is vulnerable to the true facts on its actual performance and motives. There are still many military personnel and civilians who remember the *Pasdaran's* Iran-Iraq war performance differently and can bring this truth to light, which would severely undermine the IRGC's claimed historical foundation for its current behavior.

The asymmetric warfare doctrine that Hassan Abbassi and Major General Jafari developed and the *Pasdaran* is now implementing also provides exploitable vulnerabilities. The acknowledged promotion of terrorism as a pillar of the strategy constitutes a clear and explicit violation of the Law of Armed Conflict by any interpretation of international law. This effectively isolates Iran from any external state support in the event of conflict, or limits Iran to support from a very small community of like minded states and state sponsored terrorist groups. Though willing and grateful to accept Iranian state support, its surrogates and proxies act in their own interests, with dubious reliability in the context of a larger conflict. A commentary by Mustafa Al-Sawwaf, former Editor in Chief of Hamas'

daily newspaper, the Gaza Filistin, made this clear:

> "If Iran wants to provide aid to HAMAS for the liberation of the Islamic land of Palestine, and given that Iran is an Islamic state, even though we do not share the same doctrine, HAMAS will not reject the aid and will seek to obtain it. However, if the Iranian money is aimed to form alliances, buy political positions or allegiances to this or that regime, HAMAS will not accept this. Iran understands this perfectly well, as the adage says: He who prays asks for forgiveness. If anyone is expecting to receive a [political] price in exchange for their money, then they are bound to be categorically rejected by HAMAS. I would like to point out here that Iran is not innocent in this regard. It tried and it is still trying, but it has failed and has been met with a principle stand by HAMAS regarding this matter. Perhaps it attempted to blackmail HAMAS through the money provided to the movement, but it encountered a firm HAMAS stance. It tried to use the weapon of blackmail but when it failed, it became convinced that HAMAS was holding on to its positions and that that it was not capable of giving Iran what it wanted.[16]

The terrorism pillar of Jafari's strategy relies on intimidating potential

adversaries and their supporters through the threat of terrorist activities against

non-military targets in their territories. Since September 11, 2001, states are far

more prepared to counter this threat and far more likely to respond aggressively

to an attack rather than submit to intimidation. Terrorist organizations like *Hamas*,

Lebanese *Hezballah, Khattab Hezballah* in Iraq, and the Palestinian Islamic

Jihad are well aware of this and must carefully consider their self interest before

acting on behalf of Iran's interests.

The success of Jafari's Mosaic Defense across the depth and breadth of

Iran assumes the rapid and effective mobilization of the million man *Basij* force.

While a critical strength in extending the IRGC's domestic surveillance network

across the provinces, the *Basij* remains a poorly trained and ill equipped reserve of questionable reliability. The demographics of the *Basij* are trending against the IRGC, as Iran's younger, more educated population shifts from the historically ideologically reliable rural regions to the more progressive urban regions.[17] The locally based recruiting and manning of the *Basij* units also presents an exploitable vulnerability. There are conflicting priorities among the *Basij* rank and file, who are subject to varying degrees of tribal, sect, and local loyalties. During the 1994 Qazvin riots, local IRGC and *Basij* units demonstrated independence and conflicting loyalties by refusing to fire on unarmed protestors. This required the IRGC to import *Basij* units from other provinces to quell the riots.[18] An undetermined, but significant percentage of the *Basij* rank and file have joined purely for the economic, educational, and social benefits rather than belief in the ideology or belief in the virtue of martyrdom.[19] There is opportunity to drive a wedge between the *Basij* and the IRGC by illuminating the fact that the Mosaic Defense doctrine's pillar of martyrdom applies mostly to the *Basij* rank and file and not the power brokers among the IRGC.

The IRGC is also notorious for over-reaching and hyperbole in its claims of capability and capacity. This could be a fatal flaw in its reliance on the deterrent effect of terrorist martyrdom operations. In 2005, as the head of the IRGC's Center of Strategy, Major General Jafari threatened,

> "If America were to make a mistake and carry out an attack against the sacred state of the Islamic Republic of Iran, we will set fire to its interests all over the world and will not leave it with any escape route... let the US know that if it starts a war on our soil, a war of attrition against Washington will start immediately and we will destroy all its sensitive spots... We have many martyrdom seeking forces. Each of them is the equivalent of a nuclear bomb and they are not at all afraid of death... The United States

should know that we have nuclear weapons, but they are in the hearts of our suicide bombers."[20]

Though Iran lays claim to institutionalizing martyrdom operations, it is worth noting that the vast majority of the suicide attacks in Iraq since 2003 have been at the behest of the Sunni Insurgent Groups (SIGs) rather than the Shia Extremist Groups (SEGs). Many of the SIG attacks were sectarian in nature and directly targeted Shia civilians rather than US or Coalition Forces. This does not prove that the terrorist groups Iran sponsors are no longer willing to conduct suicide attacks, but it does call into question the validity of Jafari's claim and the assumptions underpinning his strategy. Likewise, the 2011 *Basij* is not necessarily as ideologically motivated as the 1980-1988 *Basij* that fought Iraq to preserve the 1979 Revolution on Ayatollah Khomeini's behalf, when the euphoria of deposing the Shah was still fresh in their hearts and minds. Due to the potential damage and spectacular nature of any effective terrorist attack, Jafari's threat and his strategy can not and should not be taken lightly. However, the strategy assumes that the adversary will either submit or lose the will to continue based on the reliability, willingness, and effectiveness of the suicide operatives. Efforts to undermine the reliability and willingness could exploit that vulnerability and undermine the strategy.

The IRGC and *Basij's* role in crushing opposition inside Iran, in accordance with Jafari's domestic focus on preventing a 'Velvet Revolution,' is possibly the *Pasdaran's* greatest exploitable vulnerability in its military instrument of national power. The protests that followed the June 2009 presidential election extended into December 2009 and caused divisions within the IRGC. Brigadier General Mohammad Reza Mahdi, a 30 year veteran of the *Pasdaran* and formerly head of IRGC investigations to protect the regime, is now a political dissident and activist outside of Iran. In an interview with Guardian News, he claimed that over one third of the *Pasdaran* are now against the regime.

> "The current members of the Revolutionary Guard are saying that they have become very disheartened. The situation is becoming unbearable… The regime is witnessing its destruction. The regime is prepared to instill fear and insecurity into the people within Iran in order to ensure its stability. It has got to that stage. The regime is sinking."[21]

Mohammad Hussein Torkaman was the *Basij* officer responsible for security logistics for the Supreme Leader and the President during the June 2009 elections and the protests that followed. After witnessing the IRGC's methods of crushing the internal opposition, he also defected.

> "After 2009 election supreme Leader and President brought in foreign mercenaries to protect them because they were uncertain of their own security forces… The forces they had chosen to do the shooting at people were from the *Qods* Force. The majority of them are Lebanese or Palestinian. They don't speak Farsi, the Persian language. These were the ones who were given permission to open fire… They had built places within the prisons, specifically for torturing people. There's a basement in Evin prison… it was extremely bad. Disease was spreading because of the prisoners' open wounds, which had been caused by torture."[22]

Though the *Pasdaran* outwardly presents an image of a tightly knit and cohesive force that is ideologically, theologically, and politically homogenous, their role in quelling domestic revolts and crushing opposition movements has been divisive among the ranks and refutes the image of homogeneity. The IRGC members' conflicting loyalties and doubts over the *Pasdaran's* adherence to its original intended purpose are exploitable vulnerabilities in its military instrument of national power.

The Diplomatic/Political Instrument of National Power

As the IRGC is not the sole proprietor of Iran's military instrument of national power, the *Pasdaran* is also only one of many Iranian institutions that employs the diplomatic instrument of national power. Even though the IRGC is a military organization structured and commanded in a very traditional manner, it also plays a significant role in both domestic and foreign politics. Today's *Pasdaran* is far from the apolitical entity Ayatollah Khomeini envisioned in 1979.

> "I insist that the armed forces obey the laws regarding the prevention of the military forces from entering into politics, and stay away from political parties, groups and [political] fronts. The armed forces [consisting of] the military, the police force, the guards, and the *Basij* should not enter into any [political] party or groups, and steer clear from political games."[23] - Ayatollah Khomeini

Through careful and skillful cultivation, the IRGC has significantly expanded its domestic portfolio and assumed responsibilities previously reserved for the private sector, elected officials, and various ministries within the national government. This expansion should not be confused with a coup, but viewed as consolidation of power by a network of current and former IRGC commanders, with the consent and support of Supreme Leader Ali Khamenei, in accordance with his interpretation of Ayatollah Khomeni's intent for the preservation and continuation of the Islamic Revolution. Though divided by multiple camps favoring different candidates, the IRGC ultimately supported and advocated Mahmud Ahmadinejad's ascendancy to the presidency in 2005.[24] Even though

13

IRGC officers had consistently occupied multiple positions of power within the government since the 1979 revolution, Ahmadinejad accelerated and expanded IRGC and *Basij* influence by appointing *Pasdaran* personnel to 10 of the 25 cabinet ministries.[25] Former IRGC commanders already chaired and significantly influenced the powerful Assembly of Experts, responsible for overseeing the work of the Supreme Leader and amending the constitution, and the Expediency Council, responsible for ensuring legislation conforms to Islamic law, as well as screening of election candidates and certification of election results.[26] The trend of saturating the national government with IRGC personnel has continued unabated, despite President Ahmadinejad's waning influence in his second term. IRGC officers and alumni currently control or influence virtually all of the critical ministries, state media, security functions, state industry, and finance. (Refer to Appendix 1)

> "We see the ground shifting. Increasingly, the Revolutionary Guard seems to be filling the space that should be held under the Iranian system by either the clerical or the political leadership. Revolutionary Guard leaders have been assuming greater responsibility not just in the security sector and not just for the nuclear program, but in the economic and political arenas as well. The general conclusion is that there is something happening so that the political and the clerical leadership don't seem to be able to make the decisions." - US Secretary of State, Hillary Clinton[27]

The IRGC derives its far reaching domestic authority through its liberal interpretation of the Islamic Republic's constitution, specifically Article 150.

> The Islamic Revolution Guards Corps, organized in the early days of the triumph of the Revolution, is to be maintained so that it may continue in its role of guarding the Revolution and its achievements.[28]

By referencing its role in guarding the revolution, the *Pasdaran* has justified the extension of its activities to all facets of Iranian domestic and foreign politics.

Major General Mohammad Ali Jafari, Commander of the IRGC, is acutely aware of the broad authorities the Revolutionary Council vested in the IRGC. Speaking at the change of command at the Khatam al-Anbia Reconstruction Base in August, 2011, he clearly articulated his interpretation of the *Pasdaran's* charter.

> "…this goes back to IRGC's overall mission and role because many people think the IRGC is just responsible for armed defense against foreigners or domestic insecurities, but the IRGC's duty of guarding the revolution and its gains is not limited to physical defense."[29]

> "Although the IRGC was formed to protect the gains of the Islamic revolution, it is not just for opposing foreigners or maintaining domestic security because the Islamic revolution is not just threatened with new military or security threats. This was the first decade of the revolution. However in the second decade of the revolution they also saw they could not get anywhere in this way. Also the supreme leader very cleverly and wisely explained the changes in the essence of the threat to the revolution by enemies and called for preparations for IRGC involvement in various cultural and economic areas."[30]

In the context of justifying the IRGC's involvement in industry and finance, Jafari seized the opportunity to remind his multiple intended audiences that the *Pasdaran's* responsibilities reach into all aspects of governance, culture, and society. On message, Deputy IRGC Commander, Brigadier General Sardar Hossein Salami, addressed a group of *Basij* youth on 8 August, 2011 as well. "We must do all we can to safeguard the offspring of this land, who are the precious capital of Iran, against the cultural onslaught of the west and its ongoing soft war invasion."[31] The IRGC leadership, through state run media, has consistently reinforced the message that the *Pasdaran's* responsibility to protect the revolution run to the core of Iranian society.

As vetted and proven supporters of Khomeini and, more importantly, his successor Ali Khamenei, IRGC commanders and leaders have gravitated to key and critical appointed and elected positions throughout the national government. It is difficult to comprehensively and accurately list all of the key government officials associated with the IRGC and *Basij* due to the opaque nature of the republic and the multiple changes in personnel as the political tides ebb and flow. Regardless of the details of specific individuals in discreet billets, however, the overall trend has been a steady increase in IRGC power and influence within the government of the Islamic Republic of Iran. This is not to suggest that every political appointee or elected official associated with the IRGC adheres to a common, coordinated stance on every issue of policy and practice. The point is that the IRGC, more than any other entity in Iran, influences the political instrument of national power in the governance of Iran. Alumni of the IRGC and its subordinate domestic militia, the *Basij*, are ministers and/or deputy ministers of Welfare and Social Security, Islamic Culture and Guidance, Oil, Defense and Armed Forces Logistics, Industry and Mines, Commerce, Energy, and Interior. (Refer to Appendix 1, IRGC Personnel and Alumni in Key Positions)

Despite the constitutional mandate for the IRGC to adhere to duties and responsibilities defined by law,

> "The scope of the duties of this Corps, and its areas of responsibility, in relation to the duties and areas of responsibility of the other armed forces, are to be determined by law, with emphasis on brotherly cooperation and harmony among them,"[32]

The IRGC answers only to the Supreme Leader rather than an elected official, a higher military command, or any other political or clerical entity within the government of Iran. The IRGC supports and advocates for the Supreme Leader and Khamenei responds in kind. During the height of the 1997 student riots, twenty-four senior IRGC officers sent a letter to reformist president Mohammad Khatami, issuing an ultimatum that he take action against the protestors, or the IRGC would take matters into their own hands.[33] Supreme Leader Khamenei supported the IRGC officers rather than President Khatami, effectively establishing and reinforcing the IRGC's independence from the popularly elected chief executive. Dissident IRGC Brigadier General Mohammad Reza Madhi gave his assessment of presidential power in Iran, "Ahmadinejad has no power. He's a puppet, a plaything. He does what he's told. No one has any belief in him. He has no power."[34]

The *Pasdaran* owes its current status and level of political influence to the patronage of the Supreme Leader, Ali al Khamenei, and the support of his policies by the Assembly of Experts, which is also dominated by *Pasdaran* alumnus Akbar Hashemi Rafsanjani. At the age of 72, having designated no apparent successor, Khamenei has not yet secured the IRGC's political position beyond his tenure. This is a vulnerability for the IRGC, which has consolidated its power through influence and patronage in the Assembly of Experts, the Council of Guardians, and the Expediency Council. A significant political shift resulting from the designation of a more moderate or reformist successor to Khamenei would significantly threaten the IRGC's current political position. Overt interference in the process of selecting Khamenei's successor could significantly undermine the *Pasdaran's* legitimacy among both the population and the clerics responsible for choosing the next Supreme Leader. Factionalism within the IRGC would be more apparent and internal alliances of temporary convenience would be more tenuous.

The political posturing during the Ahmadinejad presidency has also exposed factions and fractures among the IRGC's senior leadership. Though the IRGC and its alumni played a large role in securing Ahmadinejad's victory in 2005, it is equally important to note that four other candidates with strong IRGC credentials ran against Ahmadinejad, including Akbar Hashemi Rafsanjani and former IRGC commander Mosen Rezai. Though legally banned from politics, factions within the IRGC chose sides, with Ahmadinejad and his base of *Basij* support emerging the victor. This divisive election drove wedges between IRGC leadership and *Pasdaran* rank and file, as well as between the IRGC and *Basij*. Rafsanjani himself accused the IRGC of election fraud and promised "divine retribution" for those involved.[35] Rafsanjani and Rezai, the *Pasdaran* alumni who lost in the 2005 election, remain politically influential and maintain their own core of IRGC supporters. Rafsanjani is today the Chair of the Expediency Council and an influential member of the council of Experts. He is also one of Iran's most wealthy men, which gives him economic as well as political influence. IRGC leadership must take care not to alienate Rafsanjani or multiple other IRGC alumni belonging to various factions. The 2005 election clearly demonstrated that the IRGC's key leaders and key alumni are not a monolithic body united in matters of strategy, policy, or politics. This is an exploitable vulnerability, especially as President Ahmadinejad's influence and support from the ageing Supreme Leader wanes in the run up to the 2012 parliamentary and 2013 presidential elections.

For very different reasons, the IRGC again ensured Ahmadinejad's victory over reformist candidate Mir Hussein Musavi in the 2009 presidential elections. In what has been generally assessed a fraudulent election, the IRGC ensured that the reformist would not have the opportunity to oust IRGC alumni from key and critical ministries. Again, former *Pasdaran* Commander Mohsen Rezai ran and lost, joining Musavi in publicly accusing the regime of election fraud.[36] Despite the shared common view that the reformist opposition must not ascend, the IRGC remained split in its support of Ahmadinejad and Rezai.

The IRGC's strategy of asymmetric warfare and its open advocacy of terrorism as a pillar of this strategy have cost Iran in the international political sphere. The US Department of State, in its 2010 annual country reports on terrorism, re-designated Iran as a state sponsor of terrorism. This is in keeping with its designation since 1984. The designation triggers mandatory sanctions on economic assistance, export of dual use items, and arms sales and exports.[37] While the designation has no binding effect on governments or private entities outside the US, the formal designation is powerful in isolating a nation politically and economically. European Union and US Department of Treasury sanctions against IRGC Major Generals Jafari and Soleimani for their material support in Syria's violent actions against protestors amplify the message that there is a political and economic price to pay for the IRGC's strategy.[38] [39] This is yet another exploitable vulnerability in the IRGC's diplomatic instrument of national power. The *Pasdaran's* military strategy has a direct and negative impact on Iran's ability to employ its political and economic tools.

Perhaps the greatest vulnerability in the IRGC's involvement in the diplomatic and political instrument of national power is that it violates the stated intent of Ayatollah Khomeini, as noted previously. His vision of an ideologically pure entity dedicated to the preservation and continuation of the revolution, with strict adherence to his version of Islamic principles, has been supplanted by an entity more driven by consolidation of power unto itself than by revolutionary principles or adherence to Islam. Khomeini himself might have underestimated what the IRGC would become. Mohsen Rezai, commander of the IRGC for 16 years wrote,

> Once someone had asked Imam [Khomeini] as to why he lends
> so much support to the IRGC. The Imam had answered "why
> not?" and the interlocutor had warned him that it may result in
> staging a coup [if the IRGC became too strong]. The Imam had
> answered, "It doesn't matter; it stays in the family [if they stage a
> coup]; as they are our own guys."[40]

Khomeini himself also provided the IRGC the very useful principle of expediency or interest of the regime (*Maslahat*) taking precedence over the tenets of Islam.[41] The IRGC has taken the principle of interest of the regime, *Maslahat*, as authority to engage in acts such as terrorism and torture even though, arguably, they violate the tenets of Islam. This dichotomy is an exploitable vulnerability for the IRGC, which vociferously portrays itself as both the guardian of the revolution and the protector of Islam. As the *Basij* officer

20

responsible for security logistics for the Supreme Leader and the President during the June 2009 elections and the period of protests following them, Mohammad Hussein Torkaman, had regular access to IRGC leadership and *Pasdaran* alumni cabinet ministers. In a June 2010 interview, he assessed, "The situation is extremely bad in Iran. They claim to be a religious state, a government based on religion. Well, I can say right now that God does not exist in Iran."[42]

Dissident and/or disgruntled former IRGC members are not the only Iranians who question the *Pasdaran's* claim of religious legitimacy. Many senior respected Shia Quietist clerics in Qom do not subscribe to clerical involvement in the politics of *raison d'état.*[43] Likewise, many Sunni religious leaders and scholars disavow the *Maslaha* principle of Iran's regime preservation taking precedence over the tenets of Islam. For these and many other reasons, the IRGC's religious mandate for participation and interference in politics does not resonate well in many Arab and Muslim nations. For a nation that aspires to lead the Islamic world, this is an exploitable vulnerability.

The *Pasdaran's* internal political factionalism is its most exploitable vulnerability. Current and former IRGC officers serving as cabinet ministers and other influential appointed positions derive their political power from several different sources, some of which are competitors. President Ahmadinejad has appointed several ministers from the 1990s IRGC alumni of the Iranian University of Science and Technology as well as the IRGC officers who served with him in northwestern Iran during the war with Iraq. Some of these appointments came at the expense of individuals favored by Supreme Leader Khamenei and Ali Akbar Rafsanjani. Other IRGC officers serving in key posts owe their appointments to the Supreme Leader or to the *Pasdaran*'s independent base of political power.[44] Individual *Pasdaran* officers must carefully balance their allegiances and adjust accordingly as the internal power struggle between President Ahmadinejad and Supreme Leader Khamenei continues to play out over time. As different alliances and camps of hardliners, moderates, and pragmatists grow and vie for power and influence, reformers have the opportunity to divide and defeat those camps in detail. This is a vulnerability that can most likely only be exploited by the citizens of Iran through free and fair elections and legal processes rather than by foreign intervention or overt support of opposition movements. Nothing more effectively unites a divided entity like the IRGC than a common enemy.

The Information Instrument of National Power

To justify its expansive role in Iranian society and to support the maintenance of its considerable influence on domestic politics, the IRGC employs multiple mechanisms to produce, disseminate, control, and screen information as it implements this instrument of national power inside the borders of Iran. In short, control of the population requires control of the information the people send and receive. The IRGC has expanded the Revolutionary Council's mandate to *train subordinate IRGC personnel in moral, ideological, and politico-military matters* to include training and enforcement of *Pasdaran* morals and ideology across the entire population. On August 3, 2011, Vice Regent Hojjat ol-Eslam Ali Saidi explained the IRGC's role in politics and culture. He reported that

22

the IRGC employs 5000 political guides and the *Basij* employs 7000 political guides to bolster IRGC spiritual and insight foundations. Saidi reinforced the IRGC's cultural responsibility, "Guarding, reinforcing, and protecting the foundations and high values of the Islamic revolution are among the genuine missions of the IRGC."[45]

The indoctrination of IRGC and *Basij* members centers on four principles: religion, obedience to the Supreme Leader, revolutionary character, and fellowship in a people's army.[46] When he assumed command of the IRGC in 2007, Major General Jafari reoriented the *Pasdaran* to counter what he assessed to be Iran's greatest national security concern: an internal 'Velvet Revolution' supported by external actors. He assessed that internal threats in the form of reformist movements and student protests posed a greater threat to the regime than conventional attack by a hostile nation. In order to enhance unity of command, unity of purpose, and unity of ideology, he requested and received formal control of the *Basij*. Jafari established 600 *Basij* Battalions and formally expanded the *Basij's* social and cultural roles, extending the IRGC's reach into every province while expanding its influence in the rural sectors.[47] Through an extensive system of incentives to include jobs, low interest loans, university attendance, and monetary compensation, the *Basij* attracts and enlists its rank and file, then implements its indoctrination in return for the benefits.[48]

Complementary to the entry level indoctrination process is the more sophisticated IRGC university system and the other institutions of higher education that it influences. Two prominent universities are Martyr Mahallati

University in Qom and Seyyed Al-Shohada Educational Center in Tabriz, which train IRGC officers and instructors in ideology and politics.[49] After the war with Iraq, the Imam Sadeq University was established in 1989, to provide the *Basij* access to higher education while promoting the values of the Islamic Republic in politics, economics, society, and education.[50]

IRGC owned or controlled cyber outlets naturally support its system of indoctrination and political/ideological education. Of the twenty seven Basij web sites, ten are dedicated to *Basij* students and scholars and three are dedicated to *Basij* professors. Additionally, six state universities maintain government sponsored websites, which are strictly controlled.[51] This overwhelming ideological virtual presence counters what the IRGC perceives as the threat of subversive ideas and impure ideology available to students and faculty in academia via the global information grid. The utilization of social media to organize and direct uprisings throughout the Middle East in 2011's Arab Spring reinforced the IRGC's premise that control of information, both proactively and reactively, is critical to maintaining the regime and the ideological purity of the revolution.

Proactively, the IRGC and *Basij* indoctrinate their own personnel and the population writ large in an effort to reinforce the ideological and political beliefs of the *Pasdaran.* The outreach to the universities and to the growing population of well educated students who would otherwise seek access to the information and ideas available on the global information grid is an example of the IRGC's employment of the informational instrument of national power to counter the trends that have led to uprisings across the region. As another initiative that could be used as a proactive information control measure or as an access portal to Iranian citizens' communications, Ali Asghar Ansari, vice president of Iran's Technology and Information Organization, announced on September 8, 2011, that Iranian citizens will be required to have an email address on a government owned and controlled network, *iran.ir*, in order to electronically access government services.[52] This amounts to compulsory registration and participation in order to access vital government services. This modern adaptation of a common population control measure also provides a cyber pathway through which the IRGC can collect information on citizens it suspects of being subversive.

There are countless examples of reactive measures taken by the IRGC and *Basij* dominated Ministry of Islamic Culture and Guidance to control information and influence the domestic population. According to the Committee to Protect Journalists, an international organization dedicated to freedom of the press, Iran consistently ranks as one of the top nations for incarcerating journalists.[53] This is not a new trend and is not unique to Iran. However, the technological sophistication of Iran's reactive measures has dramatically increased. In August 2011, the Dutch internet security company DigiNotar, suffered a complex cyber attack in which 300,000 digital security certificates were stolen. Although direct attribution of this cyber attack remains elusive, a large body of circumstantial evidence suggests Iranian state sponsorship through the IRGC. According to Fox-IT, ninety nine percent of those affected were inside

Iran. Additionally, the hackers also fabricated certificates for access to intelligence services in the US, Great Britain, and Israel, as well as America Online (AOL) and Microsoft. Finally, the hackers left a cyber signature calling card in Persian Farsi, "*Janam Fadaye Rahbar*", which translates to "I will sacrifice my soul for my leader."[54] A similar attack in March 2011against digital security company Comodo has been attributed to an Iranian hacker and bore the identical signature phrase. Mehli Abdulhayoglu, Comodo's chief executive, assessed that the attacks are politically motivated and state sponsored, with the intent of creating fake sites to trick activists into thinking they are on a secure site while collecting information on their communications.[55]

The IRGC officially established its cyber army in 2005 by assuming control of three Iranian hacking groups, *Ashiyaneh*, *Shabgard*, and *Simorgh*. According to US research firm Defense Tech, the IRGC cyber army consists of 2400 full time employees, and can leverage another 1200 private hackers. Defense Tech ranks Iran among the top five nations in terms of cyber attack capability and further assesses that the *Pasdaran's* Cyber Army has offensive cyber capabilities to include traditional tools like embedded Trojans, viruses, and worms, as well as more sophisticated tools like electromagnetic pulse weapons and wireless data communications jammers.[56]

While the IRGC maintains cyber responsibility for the Islamic Republic, it also attempts to achieve a degree of separation in cyber attacks through the use of surrogates. *Ansar al Hezballah*, a hard line conservative domestic IRGC surrogate, formally announced its establishment of Cyber *Hezballah* on 1

September 2011. *Ansar al Hezballah* openly stated that the IRGC commander for

cyber defense publicly recruited hackers to break into the networks and websites

of the Iranian government's opponents. Furthermore, *Ansar al Hezballah* vowed

to conduct extensive cyber activities domestically and throughout the world.

Cyber *Hezballah* boldly outlined its core tasks:

> 1 - Recognizing and providing identification for Hezbollah cyber activists in various areas
> 2 - Holding courses and training conferences to enable active and interested forces
> 3 - Holding meetings to provide familiarization with cyber warfare tactics, holding coordination meetings among soft war officers and cyberspace activists
> 4 - Conducting group activities and creating sweeping waves using the great Hezbollah manpower potential in the net space
> 5 - Introducing, praising and reinforcing selected activists in cyberspace in various areas[57]

Hassan Abbasi, head of the IRGC's Doctrinal Analysis Center and chief architect

of the *Pasdaran's* asymmetric warfare strategy addressed one of the initial Cyber

Hezballah conferences and has been instrumental in providing guidance on the

group's activities.[58]

Recognizing the importance of the information instrument of national

power, the IRGC has invested significant effort in controlling information

domestically and externally. In addition to its efforts in the cyber sphere, the

IRGC has also attempted to control the flow of information via satellite television

transmissions into Iran. Ebrahim Bayani, deputy for intelligence of Fars

Province's IRGC Fajr Corps, claimed that Iran's enemies are attacking the

regime via the internet and satellite television,

> "One of the things that the enemy uses to separate the people from religion and to hollow out the [ruling] system consists of cultural tools and

27

utilizing corrupt Internet sites and satellite channels, which are growing like mushrooms. Creating dissoluteness and shutting down the prohibition of vice and the enjoinment of virtue in the country through a heavy assault via satellites, which more than 50 per cent of the people use today, is one of our enemies' main programs."[59]

The IRGC and *Basij* both own and operate their own news web sites and printed news publications, but also influence nominally private Iranian news forums through their placement and access in the ministry of Islamic Culture and Guidance, which is headed by a former IRGC officer. Additionally, former IRGC commander Ezatollah Zarghami directed the national broadcast network, IRIB. This network includes five national television stations as well as multiple provincial stations. Coupled with the multiple web sites and publications dedicated to propagating the IRGC's themes and messages, the *Pasdaran* has control over a significant percentage of state media.[60] IRGC commander, Major General Jafari, has been consistent in his assessment that the greatest threat to the regime is an internal 'Velvet Revolution' supported by external actors. He has also been consistent in employing, both proactively and reactively, the information instruments of national power to mitigate that threat.

There are multiple exploitable vulnerabilities in the IRGC's information instrument of national power. There are inherent contradictions in the *Pasdaran's* principles of indoctrination: religion, obedience to the Supreme Leader, revolutionary character, and fellowship in the people's army. The first contradiction pits religion against guardianship. Because IRGC personnel are required to emulate the Supreme Leader, they are denied their Shia right to choose their source of emulation. This forms a militia cult of the Supreme Leader

28

rather than a people's army. The second contradiction is between revolution and religion. The traditional Iranian Shia Quietist interpretation of Islam promotes separation of politics and religion, which is completely antithetical to the IRGC's doctrine of the inseparability of politics and religion. The third flaw in the indoctrination principles is religion's role in a people's army. The increasingly secular growing urban population that comprises much of the resource pool for the people's army does not completely subscribe to the theology and ideology the IRGC propagates. Reliance on the rural population for the rank and file of the geographically organized and resourced IRGC and *Basij* is not sustainable. As the IRGC attempts to force its theology and politics on the urban youth, it alienates itself from a growing segment of the population.[61]

With the growing population of urban educated youth hungry for access to information via means available to most other nations around the world, the IRGC is hard pressed to close all ingress avenues for information it deems subversive. The proliferation of the internet and satellite television has outpaced the IRGC's and the Ministry of Islamic Culture and Guidance's ability to monitor, censure, and block unapproved content. Control and manipulation of information in the 21st century's cyber sphere is virtually impossible. Despite the IRGC's efforts to control information, social media has provided a portal increasingly being used by the oppressed opposition. Through Facebook and Twitter, an anonymous woman's account of her detention, torture, and rape by a regime interrogator following the disputed 2009 elections has been viewed more than 75,000 times.

"Death was my first wish. I wanted it to be over. I wanted to die. No one came to look for me. No one knew when they were raping me, or when they were burning me with cigarettes… All I had done was give one vote and that was to Mousavi. A vote that was never counted."[62]

This account and multiple other anonymous allegations are impossible to verify and subject to regime criticism as propaganda sponsored by third parties instigating the 'Velvet Revolution' the IRGC is intent on preventing. However, reformists and oppositionists have harnessed a powerful tool to disseminate information that would otherwise be censored or blocked.

Even within the IRGC's official news sites, exploitable vulnerabilities have surfaced as the *Pasdaran* has struggled to control and censure content. Javad Moghimi was a photo journalist for IRGC press agency, Fars News in 2009. He recounted his experience during the protests following the presidential election in June, "They told us not to take photographs, and said that they are not responsible if anything happens to you. We will not back you up and we will even testify against you and claim that you are spies." Modhimi disobeyed orders and photographed the protests, then fled to Turkey. His images, which the IRGC did not want exposed, made the cover of Time Magazine. Even though the IRGC arrested 39 journalists during the uprising, over 80 fled and took with them the images and information about the true state of turmoil in Iran.[63] This is only one example of the IRGC's inability to completely control the information instrument of national power. The proliferation of communications technology and the rise of social media in the form of Facebook, Twitter, YouTube, and many other outlets make attempts to control and shape information increasingly futile. Exposure and illumination of the truth is the greatest exploitation of the IRGC's vulnerability in this instrument of national power.

The IRGC's implementation of Jafari's strategy of asymmetric warfare, both domestically and abroad, creates exploitable vulnerabilities in Iran's information instrument of national power as well. Just as the military application of terrorism as a pillar of the asymmetric strategy has negative consequences on the diplomatic instrument, the employment of cyber attack in support of the information instrument has legal ramifications. If the IRGC's Cyber Army is found, within reasonable doubt, to be responsible for attacking DigiNotar in order to facilitate collection of information on Iranian citizens within its borders, the *Pasdaran* will have violated international law. Furthermore, under generally accepted international legal protocols, the government of Iran is responsible for preventing attacks emanating from within its borders. Iran is also responsible for stopping the attacks and punishing the perpetrators, even if conducted by an entity not officially affiliated with the government. Cyber *Hezballah*, by its very existence, is a violation of the protocols guiding behavior in the cyber domain. The IRGC's affiliation with or tacit support of malevolent cyber operators in support of its asymmetric warfare strategy exposes the *Pasdaran's* abuse of the information instrument of national power and invites proportional retribution from the victims, whether they be individuals, multinational corporations, or states. In January of 2010, Iranian hackers attacked *Baidu*, a Chinese search engine. Chinese hackers responded in kind, attacking multiple Iranian web sites in retaliation, sending Iran a reminder that China's cyber capability far exceeds Iran's.[64]

The Economic Instrument of National Power

The IRGC's expansion beyond the roles and tasks traditionally associated with military or security services is most pronounced in its dominant role in Iran's economy. Speaking at the change of command at the *Khatam ol-Anbia* Base Complex, IRGC commander Jafari bluntly summarized his position, "The IRGC must play a leading role in the nation's economic fronts."[65] Referencing the IRGC's role in the Iran-Iraq war, Jafari further rationalized the IRGC's economic responsibilities,

> "The IRGC actually goes into areas of activity the other sectors cannot do, as in the imposed war where because of the extent of the front and the army's ability at that time, the IRGC had the duty to go on the battlefield with all its being. We are doing the same thing today in economic areas."[66]

Articles 150 and 44 of the Islamic Republic of Iran's constitution provide the legal basis from which the IRGC derives its authority for involvement in the economy.

> Article 150: The Islamic Revolution Guards Corps, organized in the early days of the triumph of the Revolution, is to be maintained so that it may continue in its role of guarding the Revolution and its achievements. The scope of the duties of this Corps, and its areas of responsibility, in relation to the duties and areas of responsibility of the other armed forces, are to be determined by law, with emphasis on brotherly cooperation and harmony among them.[67]

> Article 44: The economy of the Islamic Republic of Iran is to consist of three sectors: state, cooperative, and private, and is to be based on systematic and sound planning. The state sector is to include all large-scale and mother industries, foreign trade, major minerals, banking, insurance, power generation, dams and large-scale irrigation networks, radio and television, post, telegraph and telephone services, aviation,

shipping, roads, railroads and the like; all these will be publicly owned and administered by the State.[68]

Leveraging its self proclaimed popularity and influence after the Iran-Iraq war, the *Pasdaran* initially entered the economic realm under the auspices of guiding the reconstruction efforts. They have steadily expanded their influence with the support and approval of the Supreme Leader. The IRGC's influence spans virtually all sectors of the economy. *Khatam ol-Anbia*, Persian for "Seal of the Prophet," is the largest contracting business within a vast network owned and/or controlled by the IRGC. The IRGC owns and operates multiple port facilities and operates its own banking system. From 2005 to 2010, the IRGC and its affiliates won 750 oil, gas, and construction contracts. In September 2009, the IRGC purchased a 50% controlling interest in Iran Telecommunications Company, complementing its information instrument of national power with an economic instrument.[69] While it is difficult to accurately capture all of the companies under the IRGC's business portfolio, appendices 2-5 from Ali Alfoneh's June 2010 article in Middle East Outlooks provides and extensive list of companies and investment institutes entirely or partially owned by the IRGC.[70] (See Appendices 2-5)

In 2005, Supreme Leader Khamenei directed "privatization" of 25% of Iran's publicly held assets, amounting to $110-120 billion worth of assets going to cooperatives, which were owned or controlled by the government. This effectively transferred ownership and control from one public sector to another. Through its complex network of foundations and their subsidiary banks, assisted by generous subsidies, the IRGC has diligently expanded its business holdings at a deep

33

discount. The true private sector only gained 19% of the "privatized" public assets, while the cooperatives consumed 68% of the resources. The IRGC has systematically militarized rather than privatized the Iranian economy.[71]

By far, the IRGC's greatest economic instrument is its influence over the energy sector, which accounts for over 80% of the regime's revenue.[72] As commander of the powerful *Khatam ol-Anbia*, IRGC Brigadier General Rostam Ghasemi displaced international oil companies Shell and Total to take full control of the South Pars oil and gas fields, securing no-bid contracts for multiple phases of the fields' development.[73] In August 2011, the Islamic Republic's elected parliament, the *Majles*, confirmed the nomination of IRGC Brigadier General Rostam Ghasemi to be the nation's oil minister. This was despite the fact that Ghasemi was already the subject of US and international sanctions for his association with terrorist activities. Iran currently holds the rotating position of president of OPEC, effectively placing an IRGC officer in a position to employ Iran's economic instrument of national power both domestically and globally in the critical energy sector of the world economy.[74]

The IRGC's overt activity in the Iranian economy is only one of the *Pasdaran's* tools for implementing the economic instrument of power. The IRGC influences or controls a vast network of *bonyads*, or foundations though which it exerts its economic and social influence. These foundations account for 20% of Iran's Gross Domestic Product.[75] In the regime's post revolutionary consolidation, it assumed control of the multiple foundations the Shah had established as informal and extra-legal networks. While officially a non-governmental organization, the Foundation for the Oppressed, *Bonyad Mostazafan*, is the nation's largest and is chaired by Mohammad Forouzandeh, a former IRGC officer. This massive foundation has over 350 subordinate companies and is diversified throughout the agricultural, transportation, tourism, and industrial sectors of the economy. Its agricultural subsidiary alone has an additional 115 companies. Reportedly, 50% of the foundation's profits go to aid to the needy, provide low interest loans to the poor, and pay pensions. The remainder is available for re-investment in the foundation's companies or for the acquisition of additional companies.[76] Through economic favoritism, the IRGC has employed the *bonyads* to displace independent private industry and prevent it from re-emerging. This economic instrument reinforces the political and information instruments by providing social security, social mobility, and popular mobilization.[77]

The gray and black markets comprise a significant sector of Iran's economy. The IRGC, through its ownership of ports, its influence over airlines, and its nearly immune status among Iranian law enforcement services, has the means and opportunity to play a dominant role in the black and gray market economy. There are multiple motives for this involvement: personal profit for senior officers, funding and acquisition of weapon systems subject to sanctions, bribery of political and clerical officials in order to maintain and increase the IRGC's economic and political position, support covert initiatives abroad, support the IRGC's nuclear research program, provision of financial support to IRGC veterans and their families, and growth of the *Basij* through financial incentives.[78]

By militarizing an enormous percentage of Iran's national economy, the IRGC has built a powerful tool to complement and enhance its ability to influence the military, information, and diplomatic/political instruments of national power. It has also created numerous exploitable vulnerabilities. Though the IRGC diligently employs its information instruments to mask the truth and obfuscate the facts, the mass of the Iranian people know that their economy is in deep trouble and that their economic prospects for the future are not favorable. The IRGC sends conflicting signals through its information instrument by alternately blaming the US and US sanctions for Iran's economic woes, while claiming that the sanctions are ineffective and futile. Janes Sentinel Security, in August 2011, assessed that the Iranian economy will need to create 700,000 jobs annually to meet the demand of a growing supply of young workers. With both unemployment and inflation at over 25%, Janes assessed that the economy can not meet the challenge.[79]

As commander of the *Khatam ol-Anbia* construction base, Brigadier General Rostam Ghasemi summarized the IRGC's view of direct foreign investment in Iran, "This base must become a replacement for the large foreign companies."[80] In a world economy that is increasingly integrated and interdependent, the IRGC leadership is moving Iran's economy in an entirely different direction that is destined to further isolate and alienate Iran from other nations. In keeping with Jafari's intent to become completely self sufficient, with all critical sectors of the economy under the control or influence of the IRGC, Iran has denied itself any of the benefits of the global market beyond the energy sector. This is a distinct vulnerability in the IRGC's economic instrument of national power.

Sanctions have significantly affected Iran's militarized economy. The oil sector is highly dependent on income from oil and gas exports to India, which accounts for 17% of Iran's exports.[81] India, however, has begun to diversify its import sources in order to reduce its reliance on Tehran. Sanctions against IRGC affiliated banks have made it difficult, if not impossible for India and other nations to pay their oil debts to Iran. Various reports indicate that South Korea could owe as much as $4.7 billion and China as much as $30 billion that they can not pay due to the sanctions.[82]

The *Pasdaran's* extra-legal economic activity has not gone un-noticed by Iran's elected parliamentarians. In reference to the IRGC's black and gray market activities, *Majlis* member Ali Ghanbari openly criticized the *Pasdaran*,

> "...unfortunately, one third of the imported goods are delivered through the black market, underground economy, and illegal jetties. Appointed institutions [by Supreme Leader Khamenei] that don't obey the [rules of] the government and have control over the means of power [violence]; institutions that are mainly military, are responsible [for those illegal activities]."[83]

Former *Majlis* Speaker and reformist cleric Mehdi Karrubi accused the IRGC of running 60 extralegal jetties without proper governmental supervision. Another Member of Parliament quantified his estimate of the IRGC's illicit economic activity, "invisible jetties . . . and the invisible hand of the mafia control 68 percent of Iran's entire exports."[84] As a reformist candidate for the presidency and an outspoken critic of the regime and the *Pasdaran*, Mehdi Karrubi remains under house arrest.

Corruption and personal enrichment invites contempt and competition among the senior IRGC officers, and creates an opportunity for a wedge between the leadership and the rank and file of the organization. The slow deterioration of the once influential Bazaar merchant middle class through the IRGC's control of the underground economy and its militarization of the private sector has also created a vulnerability by alienating a large segment of the population accustomed to a tradition of relatively free enterprise. In a formal letter to the government, 29 private businessmen openly questioned the constitutionality as well as the effectiveness of the IRGC's economic activities,

> "Responsibilities [of the military and civilian institutions] are well defined in the Constitution. [Moreover] the goal of the "Next 20 Years' Economic Projection," is to make the government smaller. [We ask the question] whether it makes sense economically and technically, to award [all the] large scale projects to the military or paramilitary organizations?"[85]

The Jerusalem Force Exercising All Instruments of National Power

The IRGC's domestic focus does not suggest a lack of involvement in Iran's external affairs. Through its subordinate *Qods* (Jerusalem) Force, the IRGC exercises all instruments of national power on Iran's behalf. The Jerusalem Force acts as a diplomatic corps, an intelligence/information service, an irregular warfare proponent, and a non-governmental organization.

The Jerusalem Force has long been assessed as functionally independent from the IRGC hierarchy. In January 2011, Supreme Leader Khamenei promoted the *Qods* Force commander, Khassim Soleimani, to Major General, the highest rank in Iran's armed forces since the Iran-Iraq war ended. In rank he is equal to the *Pasdaran* Commander, Major General Jafari.[86] In practice, Soleimani also ultimately answers only to Kamenei, giving the Jerusalem Force Commander the same direct and frequent access to the Supreme Leader that the IRGC Commander enjoys.[87] In 2003, Supreme Leader Khamenei paid Soleimani homage usually reserved for the deceased by describing him as, "...someone who was martyred at the front on numerous occasions and is a living martyr of the revolution."[88] Based on the importance of martyrdom in revolutionary Iran's interpretation of Shia Islam, this complement from Khamenei is indicative of Soleimani's standing and referent power among the *Pasdaran*.

The IRGC's external arm's designation as the Jerusalem Force is symbolic and significant as well. A popular image during the Iran-Iraq war depicted an arrow stretching from Iran, through Iraq's Shiite holy city of Karbala to the Dome of the Rock in Jerusalem. The image and its accompanying slogan, "the path to Jerusalem runs through Karbala" suggests Iran's manifest destiny to unite the Islamic world under Shia leadership in order to take the Islamic holy city of Jerusalem from Israel.[89] This defines the *Qods* Force's struggle against imperialism and Zionism.

The Jerusalem Force is Iran's primary practitioner of irregular warfare outside its borders. In keeping with Iran's strategy of asymmetric warfare previously discussed within the context of the military instrument of national power, the *Qods* Force employs all instruments of national power in support of this strategy. The Jerusalem Force performs functions normally executed by officers of the diplomatic corps, the foreign ministry, the national intelligence service, the ministry of defense, and the ministry of finance in most other nations.

As commander of the Jerusalem Force, Major General Khassim Soleimani, wields extraordinary power and influence. In a think tank discussion forum in 2010, General David Petraeus related a message Soleimani had sent him in 2008.

> "He said, "General Petraeus, you should know that I, Kassim Soleimani, control the policy for Iran with respect to Iraq, Lebanon, Gaza, and Afghanistan. And indeed, the ambassador in Baghdad is a Qods Force member. The individual who's going to replace him is a Qods Force member."

> General Petraeus elaborated,

> "Now, that makes diplomacy difficult if you think that you're going to do the traditional means of diplomacy by dealing with another country's Ministry of Foreign Affairs because in this case, it is not the ministry. It's not Mottaki who controls the foreign policy, again, for these countries, at least. It is, again, a security apparatus, the *Qods* Force, which is also carrying out other activities."[90]

In the opinion of several prominent Iraqi politicians, *Qods* Force Commander Soleimani wields inordinate power and influence. According to Mowaffak al-Rubaie Iraq's former national security minister, "He is the most powerful man in Iraq, without question. Nothing gets done without him."[91] Saleh al-Mutlaq, an influential Iraqi Sunni politician, said, "His power comes straight from Khamenei. It bypasses everyone else, including Ahmadinejad."[92] In reference to the significant casualties US Forces sustained in June 2011, the Director General of the intelligence division in Iraq's Ministry of Interior, Hussein Kamal assessed,

> "It is clear that the *al-Quds* Force is responsible. There has been a systematic flow of weapons into Iraq for the past eight years. Of course they try to say it is not state-sponsored. But when weapons are flowing from the borders of a sovereign state, it is very clear where the blame lies.

They are destructive weapons and they cannot deny the responsibility for them."[93]

The Jerusalem Force also implements the economic instrument of national power in Iraq. *Qods* Force member and head of the Iran-Iraq economic commission, Hassan Kazemi Qom, is responsible for implementing Iran's plan to increase its energy sector trade with Iraq from $6 billion to $20 billion over the next five years. This is in addition to economic initiatives at the provincial and local level. This economic influence, coupled with the *Qods* Force's sponsorship of Shia militia groups *Asaib al Haq*, the Promise Day Brigades, and *Khattab Hizballah*, demonstrate the *Qods* Force's ability to implement the economic instrument of national power in support of the military instrument abroad through sponsorship and training of surrogates and proxies.[94]

The Jerusalem Force also has a long history of implementing Iran's military, information, and economic instruments of national power in Lebanon, through its surrogate, Lebanese *Hezballah* (LH). Through the *Qods* Force, Iran has re-armed LH with over 25,000 rockets and 500 *Zelzal* rockets since the 2006 LH conflict with Israel. With a range of 186 miles, the *Zelzal* rockets give LH a capability and considerable capacity to strike Tel Aviv.[95] In concert with the military instrument, the Jerusalem Force also implemented the economic and information instruments by providing LH at least $150 million to distribute to Shia supporters whose homes were damaged during the 2006 Israeli conflict. The US State Department's Terrorism Report for 2008 assessed that Iranian aid to LH exceeded $200 million that year.[96]

The advent of the Arab Spring in 2011 has given Soleimani justification for expanding the *Qods* Force's diplomatic portfolio to several other nations as well. In a May 2011 speech to students at the Haqqani Theological Seminary, Soleimani stated, "Today, Iran's victory or defeat no longer takes place in Mehran and Khorramshahr. Our boundaries have expanded and we must witness victory in Egypt, Iraq, Lebanon, and Syria. This is the fruit of the Islamic revolution."[97] Consistent with the IRGC doctrine of asymmetric warfare and the IRGC's employment of all instruments of national power, Soleimani and the *Qods* Force are waging intensive political, informational, and economic warfare, in addition to sponsoring and training surrogates, proxies, and terrorists. Through its intervention in Syria, the Jerusalem Force and its commander offered a critical exploitable vulnerability that the US Government exposed. President Obama signed Executive Order 13573 on 18 May, 2011, condemning Soleimani and the *Qods* Force for its role in violating human rights by assisting the Asad regime in suppressing Syrian civilians. Assistant Secretaries of State Posner and Feltman testimony to the US Congress was unambiguous,

> "It is no coincidence both Iran and Syria have responded to their citizens with similar contempt and brutal tactics. As the latter designation shows, we know that the Syrians have employed Iranian help in curbing dissent. This has exposed a strident hypocrisy on the part of the Iranian regime, which has tried unsuccessfully to take credit for democratic movements in Egypt and elsewhere and laud protesters when it suited its strategic interests, but has materially helped the Syrian government crush its own protestors in order to preserve their ally. The Iranian regime's false narrative is further exposed even as the regime continues to smother its own domestic opposition."[98]

The US State Department refuted Iran's and Soleimani's attempt to hijack the Arab Spring movement by taking credit for regime changes around the region while supporting the repressive Syrian regime in its human rights abuses against its own peacefully protesting citizens.

The US Department of State's 2010 annual report on terrorism states that the *Qods* Force is Iran's "primary mechanism for cultivating and supporting terrorists abroad." The report cites the Jerusalem Force's training and provision of lethal aid to insurgents and militants in both Afghanistan and Iraq, its expenditure of hundreds of millions of dollars in support of *Hezballah* in Lebanon, and its training of thousands of fighters in camps inside Iran.[99] On May 17, 2011, the US Treasury Department sanctioned Major General Soleimani and his officer in charge of training and operations, Mohsen Chizari, for being "the conduit for Iranian material support to the GID (Syrian intelligence service accused of repressing its citizens)"[100] The duplicity of Iran's policy of intervention in Lebanon, Iraq, and Syria is an exploitable vulnerability in the region as well as inside Iran.

The Jerusalem Force has many of the same exploitable vulnerabilities as the rest of the *Pasdaran*. As the IRGC's external practitioner, the *Qods* Force has some unique vulnerabilities as well. Current Defense Minister and former Jerusalem Force commanding general, Ahmad Vahidi, is subject to an Interpol Red Notice for his alleged involvement in multiple bombings and assassinations on three continents. His ability to travel is limited to those nations which lack an extradition treaty or refuse to honor the associated indictments. Major General Soleimani could very well fall into the same situation, given the US and European Union sanctions already levied against him. As practitioners of asymmetric warfare outside their borders, *Qods* Force Officers are also at risk of being exposed, killed, or captured. In 2006 and 2007, Coalition Forces captured one Lebanese *Hezballah* senior officer and several *Qods* Force officers operating inside Iraq, exposing them and their malevolent activities to the Iraqis and the world.[101]

The *Qods* Force practice of placing its personnel in Iranian embassies as diplomats, as articulated by Major General Soleimani to General Petraeus, creates a vulnerability in Iran's diplomatic instrument of national power. By delegating responsibility for implementing foreign policy to the *Qods* Force rather than a trained and experienced foreign service, Iran has sidelined its professional diplomats in favor of the IRGC and its agenda. There is a risk of *Pasdaran* and *Qods* Force policy dictating Iranian national foreign policy without regard for unintended consequences or second and third order effects.

Conclusions

Through the *Pasdaran's* pervasive influence and active employment of all instruments of national power, the IRGC has become the government of Iran's center of gravity not only in terms of national security, but also for all other aspects of governance. In military terms, an adversary cannot currently defeat the *Pasdaran* without changing the regime, and cannot change the regime without defeating the *Pasdaran*. Despite its pervasive influence via its extensive network of current and former IRGC political heavyweights, its carefully crafted information control and manipulation tools, its primacy over all critical national security tasks, and its elaborate economic enterprise, the *Pasdaran* has significant exploitable vulnerabilities in each instrument of national power. (Reference Chart 1, Summary)

Major General Jafari's assessment that the greatest threat to the regime is that of a 'Velvet Revolution' coming from within the nation's population, supported by an external actor or actors, is likely correct. Sufficient popular support is critical to preserving the regime. Widespread popular dissent and demand for change is equally critical for regime change. The US or any other potential adversary would likely bolster the regime and validate the IRGC's growing role in preserving the regime and propagating the revolution if a significant percentage of Iranian citizens actively oppose or passively observe a coordinated attempt to change the regime. Even with widespread support from a significant percentage of the population, an attempt to defeat the *Pasdaran* and/or change the regime would require a sustained and disciplined whole of governments approach over an extended period. Note that 'governments' is plural, meaning that no single nation acting independently could achieve regime change or fundamentally change the IRGC even if that nation efficiently and effectively employed all instruments of its own national power. A significant advantage goes to the defender, the IRGC, and the status quo in this case.

Recommendations

Even though IRGC defense doctrine emphasizes soft power and asymmetric warfare over the technological and physical aspects traditionally associated with kinetic warfare, no potential adversary should underestimate the necessity of maintaining a credible kinetic deterrent. In its autonomous application of calibrated violence consistent with Jafari's asymmetric warfare doctrine, the *Pasdaran* and/or its proxies could easily miscalculate the second and third order effects of their malevolent behavior and employment of terrorism, producing unacceptable unintended consequences. Potential adversaries and competitors must remain cognizant of this and should be prepared to respond proportionally and appropriately in order to establish and reinforce the relevance of deterrence.

Regardless of intent or lack of intent to change the Islamic Republic of Iran's current regime, support of oppositionists and reformists is consistent with the US policies of support for human rights and emerging democracies. The US has the capability to use its own hard and soft instruments of national power to encourage other similarly inclined nations to pledge and deliver their support as well. Accurate and timely information, widely and effectively disseminated, is critical in any efforts to influence the *Pasdaran* or the regime. In order to substantively back claims of malevolent IRGC behavior, the US and allied nations will need to carefully consider declassifying and sharing sensitive intelligence information while balancing the desire to protect sensitive sources and collection methods. The information supporting US claims and justifying US actions must withstand scrutiny from not only the international community, but also the sophisticated information control, distortion, and dissemination architecture the *Pasdaran* has carefully cultivated over the last three decades to deny the Iranian population access to the truth.

Diplomatic/Political

As state sponsors of terrorism in accordance with the IRGC's asymmetric warfare doctrine, Iran's diplomatic instrument of national power is extremely vulnerable. The US and other nations should continue to condemn the support of terrorist organizations and discourage any other nation from entering into bilateral agreements with the terrorist state of Iran. At the far end of the diplomatic spectrum is a political ultimatum requiring other nations to publicly declare their support for Iran and its policies of promoting terrorism, abusing human rights, and repressing its population; or to join in a coalition of like minded nations condemning these practices and refusing to recognize the Iranian regime that implements these unacceptable policies. A tangible first step is to continue to indict key IRGC leaders, restrict their international travel, and seize their assets held abroad. European Union arrest warrants should accompany every EU sanction against *Pasdaran* leadership. The US could then leverage the soft power of the EU member nations to secure cooperation from additional nations currently unwilling to arrest and/or extradite IRGC senior officers like Jafari, Vahidi, Ghasemi, and Soleimani. The US State Department should continue to encourage other nations to recognize Iran as a state sponsor of terrorism. Declarations or demarches from Islamic nations like Turkey, Saudi Arabia, Egypt, and Pakistan would help to invalidate the IRGC's credibility as self proclaimed guardians of the faith.

Whenever and wherever the Jerusalem Force is operating behind the veil of diplomatic immunity from within Iranian embassies and consulates, the US and other nations should also carefully consider exposing this practice and these operatives. There are multiple potential negative second and third order effects in doing so, but the US and other nations have the option to overtly and openly expose the *Qods* Force, or to more discreetly inform select partner nations through diplomatic or intelligence channels.

The US can exploit the factions among the *Pasdaran* by being perfectly clear that the US is open to dialogue with responsible reformists and pragmatists who seek a mutual relationship of trust and partnership rather than conflict. To be effective, this message must be unambiguous and consistent, with multiple target audiences to include IRGC leadership, elected Iranian politicians, the *Artesh*, and the Iranian people.

Informational

If mobilizing the population of Iran is the key to either maintaining or changing the regime, the information the population receives is the key to effective mobilization. The truth is on the side of the IRGC's adversaries, both inside Iran and external to Iran. The proliferation of truth via the internet, satellite television, and social networks serves to expose and illuminate the inherent contradictions of the IRGC indoctrination effort and the abuse of its extra-legal authority to guide and regulate culture and society in Iran. The US and partners should actively support and encourage all of these information venues and aggressively oppose and expose the IRGC Cyber Army and surrogate Cyber *Hezballah's* virtual terrorism. The *Pasdaran's* information instrument of national power, like its military instrument, depends largely on the calculus of intimidation and calibrated violence, counting on both the Iranian population and other nations to avoid confrontation out of fear of what harm the regime might do. Constant exposure and illumination of IRGC abuses of Iran's informational tools, coupled with proportional and appropriate state retaliation against reasonably attributable attacks could affect or change the IRGC's calculus. The United States, other nations, and the civilian commercial sector with experience and expertise in cyber security can and should aggressively work together to protect infrastructure, information, and networks from Iranian cyber attack. Likewise, the US should use its available soft power tools to share information and training support on cyber security best practices with other susceptible nations to proactively deter and mitigate the IRGC Cyber Army's intimidation.

The US and its allies must also communicate, through all available means, with the nearly 80 million citizens of Iran, constantly reinforcing the message that US Secretary of State Hillary Clinton articulated in 2010, "We want to send a clear message that it's not about the Iranian people; this is about the Revolutionary Guard."[102] There must be a proactive, sustained campaign to expose and illuminate the *Pasdaran's* malevolent behavior both inside Iran and around the world, and to inform the Iranian people of the consequences associated with this unacceptable behavior.

Military

The US and allied nations' militaries should maintain technical and physical regional superiority, providing a credible deterrent to the IRGC threat of asymmetric warfare and terrorism, as well as malevolent behavior in neighboring nations. Through theater security cooperation in multiple geographic combatant commands, the US Departments of Defense, State, Justice, and Treasury should also continue to support improvement in counter-terrorism capability and capacity among allied nations in order to deter the *Pasdaran's* implementation of terrorism as a pillar of its military doctrine and strategy. Within the United States Central Command area of responsibility, specifically the nations bordering the Arabian Gulf and Strait of Hormuz; military sales, training, exercises, and intelligence sharing should all be coordinated to counter the IRGC's asymmetric warfare doctrine and its naval swarm tactics. The US could also make a case for declaring the entire *Pasdaran* and *Basij* terrorist organizations, exempt from the protections normally afforded uniformed armed forces under the Geneva Conventions and the Laws of Armed Conflict due to both organizations' sponsorship and training of the terrorist organizations previously noted.

Additionally, the US military should consider developing a campaign plan based on exploiting the inherent flaws in Jafari's Mosaic Defense doctrine by segregating and isolating the IRGC and *Basij* from the *Artesh*, and driving a wedge between the *Pasdaran* elite leadership and the rank and file expected to martyr themselves on the IRGC's behalf. The US can make clear to the *Artesh* that there is a place for that element of Iran's armed services in a future sovereign Iran that is free from the *Pasdaran* and its leaders. The US can also communicate directly to the *Basij* that mass attrition of their rank and file is only in the best interest of the IRGC, not the US or the Iranian people.

The US and allied militaries should also consider improving the capability and capacity of their Military Information Support Operations (MISO), tailored to achieve and maintain information superiority as quickly as militaries would normally strive to achieve air superiority against a traditional adversary. The tools and skills required are not necessarily the same as those employed in Iraq and Afghanistan and can not be produced rapidly. Early investment in learning the Farsi language and understanding the Persian culture would be critical to effective employment of the military instrument of national power.

Economic

The US and allied nations should fully expose the IRGC economic enterprise to both the Iranian people and the rest of the world. Through information and intelligence sharing, the US can provide the transparency that the IRGC has obfuscated through its use and abuse of foundations, cooperatives, front companies, and the black market. The Iranian private sector bazaar middle class should be encouraged and should have full visibility of the unfair business practices the *Pasdaran* enterprise employs to enrich its elite and to finance its consolidation of power.

Economic sanctions and US Department of Treasury designations should extend to all *bonyads*, banks, and cooperatives associated with this vast network. Though currently having an effect, US unilateral sanctions are not completely effective in preventing the *Pasdaran* from generating and laundering the revenue required to maintain and expand its domestic and international influence. The US should also consider engaging regional political and economic interests like the European Union, MERCOSUR, the African Union, ASEAN, and the Gulf

Cooperation Council, as well as member nations of the World Trade Organization to honor sanctions against the entirety of the *Pasdaran's* economic enterprise.

The US and other willing nations should also aggressively support development of alternative markets and sources of oil and gas for nations dependent on Iranian imports. Coupled with economic sanctions against the IRGC economic enterprise, this could have a profound effect on the *Pasdaran's* ability to implement its economic instrument of national power.

Closing Comments

The May 2010 National Security Strategy of the United States of America states,

> "We will disrupt, dismantle, and defeat al-Qa'ida and its affiliates through a comprehensive strategy that denies them safe haven, strengthens front line partners, secures our homeland, pursues justice through durable legal approaches, and counters a bankrupt agenda of extremism and murder with an agenda of hope and opportunity."[103]

Though Osama bin Laden and Anwar al-Awlaki are dead, and al-Qa'ida has suffered substantial losses in terms of senior leadership and popular support, al-Qa'ida remains a significant threat to US national security. However, Iran, under the influence of the *Pasdaran* and its political and clerical mentors, poses a greater potential threat to US national security. As a pillar of the IRGC's military doctrine and strategy, Iran's state sponsorship of terrorism remains unacceptable, but largely unchallenged. Since September 11, 2001, the US government and willing partner nations have employed the principles of cooperative security and whole of governments implementation of the instruments of national power against al-Qa'ida. Senior leaders should leverage the lessons learned from this experience and apply them toward exploiting the

multiple vulnerabilities of the *Pasdaran* terrorist network as well.

Appendix 1: IRGC Personnel and Alumni in Key Positions[104],[105],[106]

Current and former IRGC personnel placement and access (as of 01 AUG 2011)

Mahmoud Ahmadinejad—President of the Islamic Republic of Iran, former mayor of Tehran, Basij volunteer during Iran-Iraq war

Esfandiar Rahim-Mashaei -- Ahmadinejad's Chief of Staff, established the IRGC intelligence unit in Kurdistan

Hoseyn Dehgan – Vice president, former commander of the IRGC in Lebanon and Tehran, former commander of the IRGC Air Force, former General Manager of the Cooperatives Foundation of the IRGC

Saeed Jalili—Secretary of the Supreme National Security Council and top nuclear negotiator (replacing Ali Larijani), former Basij commander

Ali Larijani—Speaker of the *Majlis*, Expediency Council member, former IRGC member, former head of state TV and radio, former SNSC representative to Khamenei

Sadegh Mahsouli —Minister of Welfare, former commander of the IRGC District 5 and Special district 6, formerly Ahmadinejad's commanding officer

Ahmad Vahidi -- Minister of Defense and Armed Forces Logistics, former Commanding General of the IRGC Qods Force

Mohammad Hoseyn Saffar-Harandi—Minister of Islamic Culture and Guidance, former IRGC deputy commander of Hormozgan province, 1980–1981; former national regional deputy commander of IRGC, 1981–1983; director of the Political Office of the IRGC, 1989–1993

Rostam Qasemi – Minister of Petroleum, former IRGC commander of Khatam ol-Anbia construction base

Mohammad Mostafa Najjar— Minister of Interior, Former Minister of Defense and Armed Forces Logistics; in General Command of Central Headquarters of IRGC Sistan va Baluchestan province; in charge of the Cooperative Office of 104 Assessing the Domestic Roles of Iran's Islamic Revolutionary Guards Corps the IRGC, 1981; former deputy director of the Warfare Group of the Ministry of the Guards Corps (Vezarat-e Sepah); member of IRGC since late 1979; membership in the board of directors of the Guards Corps Industries; creation of the Training, Treatment, and Equipment Center of the Guards Corps Hospital

Mehdi Ghazanfari —Minister of Commerce, Industries and Mines, Iran University of Science and Technology and IRGC alumnus

Aliakbar Mehrabian – Minister of Industry, Member of the Central Command Council of Student Basij, nephew of Ahmadinejad, IRGC alumnus

Ali Akbar Salehi – Minister of Foreign Affairs, IRGC associations through Iran's nuclear program

Hamidreza Hajibabayi – Minister of Education, IRGC alumnus

Kamran Daneshjou – Minister of Science and Higher Education, IRGC alumnus

Reza Taghipour Anvari -- Minister of Communications and Information Technology, IRGC association through telecommunications industry

Mohammed Abbasi – Minister of Cooperatives, IRGC alumnus
Majid Namjou—Minister of Energy, former IRGC security officer, civilian deputy of the Khatam ol-Anbia construction base
Hoseini Shahrudi—Director of the Indoctrination Bureau of the IRGC

Other Government Officials/Advisors (as of 2009)
Yahya Rahim Safavi—Assistant and senior advisor to commander-in-chief of Iranian Armed Forces (Khamenei), former commanding general of the IRGC
Mohsen Rezai—Secretary General of Expediency Council, one of the original IRGC members, former commanding general of the IRGC
Hojjat ol-Eslam Behzad Jalali— Khamenei's representative in the IRGC

University Chiefs (as of 2009)
Kelishadi—Head of Amir al-Mu'minin University
Behrouz Moradi—On faculty at Imam Hosein University; governor of Hamedan
Mohammad Mehdi Zahedi—Head of the SBO at the Science and Industry University
Mardani—Head of the Iranian SBO
Ja'far Ya'qubi—Head of the LBO

Bonyad/Media/Business Heads (as of 2009)
Mohammad Forouzandeh—Director of the Mostazafan and Janbazan Foundation; Head of the IRGC General Headquarters; Assistant Commander-in-Chief of the IRGC in Reorganizing the IRGC's three Naval, Air, and Ground Units
Brigadier General Ehtessam—Director of Hara Company
Hossein Shariatmadari—Director of *Keyhan* newspaper
Hoseyn Dehghan—Deputy to the president and director of the Martyr's foundation; former IRGC Air Force commander

Appendix 2[107]

Companies and Investment Institutes Entirely or Partially Owned by the IRGC Cooperative Foundation as of May 31, 2010

Alaleh-ye Kavir Samen al-Aemeh Cultural and Service Institution [*Moassesseh-ye Farhangi/Khadamati-ye*
Samen al-Aemeh-ye Sherkat-e Alaleh-ye Kaboud-e Kavir]

Baharan Company [*Sherkat-e Baharan*]

Bahman Group [*Gorouh-e Bahman*]

Behinesas Engineering Prefabricated Articles [*Mohandesi-ye Amadeh-ye Behinesaz*]

Chaharmahal and Bakhtiari Food Products Yeast Company [*Mavad-e Ghazayi-ye Khamir-Mayeh*
Chaharmahal Va Bakhtiari]

Housing Jihad Companies [*Sherkatha-ye Jahad-e Khaneh-sazi*]

Iran Telecommunications [*Sherkat-e Mokhaberat-e Iran*]

Isfahan Zowb-rou Company [*Sherkat-e Zowb-ro-ye Esfahan*]

Kermanshah Petrochemical Industries [*Sanaye' Petroshimi-ye Kermanshah*]

Khorasan Shadab Agricultural and Industrial Company [*Sherkat-e Kesht Va San'at-e Shadab-e Khorasan*]

Kish Atlas Commerce and Industrial Company [*Sherkat-e Bazargani Va San'ati-ye Iran Atlas-e Kish*]

Kish Bahrestan Company [*Sherkat-e Bahrestan-e Kish*]

Kowsaran Institute [*Moassesseh-ye Kowsaran*]

Maedeh Food Industries [*Sanaye' Ghazayi-ye Maedeh*]

Misagh-e Basirat Institute [*Moassesseh-ye Misagh-e Basirat*]

Mowj-e Nasr-Goster Communications Company [*Sherkat-e Mokhaberati-ye Mowj-e Nasr-Gostar*]

Navid-e Bahman Company [*Sherkat-e Navid-e Bahman*]

Ofogh-e Tos'eh-ye Saberin Engineering Company [*Mohandesi-ye Ofogh-e Tose'eh-ye Saberin*]

Omran-e Mohit Consultancy and Development Company [*Sherkat-e Andisheh Va Omran-e Mohit*]

Pars Air Services [*Sherkat-e Khadamat-e Havayi-ye Pars*]

Pre-Fabricated Light Structures Consulting Engineering Company [*Sherkat-e Mohandesin-e Moshaver-e Sazeh-ha-ye*
Pishsakhteh-ye Sabok]

Rahian-e Komeyl Commercial and Consulting Services Institute [*Moassesseh-ye Khadamat-e Bazargani/Moshaverehi-ye*
Rahian-e Komeyl]

Razmandeh Social Housing Company [*Mojtama'e Khaneh-sazi-ye Razmandeh*]

Sepahan Social Housing Company [*Sherkat-e Mojtama'e Khaneh-sazi-ye Sepahan*]

Shahab-Sang Mining Industries [*Sanaye' Ma'dani-ye Shahab-Sang*]

Shahriar-e Mahestan Investment Company [*Sherkat-e Sarmayehgozari-ye Shahriar-e Mahestan*]

Tose'eh-ye E'temad Investment Company [*Sherkat-e Sarmayehgozari-ye Tose'eh-ye E'temad*]

Yazd Bahar Wool Company [*Sherkat-e Pashmbafi-ye Bahar-e Yazd*]

Zagros Steel [*Foulad-e Zagros*] (end note, Alfoneh, The Revolutionary Guards' Looting of Iran's Economy, p9)

Appendix 3[108]

Subsidiaries of the Mehr Finance and Credit Institution
Azerbaijan Kowsar Company [*Sherkat-e Kowsar-e Azerbaijan*]
Kousha Paydar Company [*Sherkat-e Kousha Paydar*]
Mehr Ayandehnegar Commerce Services Company [*Sherkat-e Khadamat-e Bazargani-ye Ayandehnegar-e Mehr*]
Mehr Housing and Development Investment Company [*Sherkat-e Sarmayehgozari-ye Maskan Va Omran-e Mehr*]
Mehr-e Eghtesad-e Iranian Investment Company [*Sherkat-e Sarmayehgozari-ye Mehr-e Eghtesad-e Iranian*]
Tadbirgaran-e Atiyeh Company [*Sherkat-e Tadbirgaran-e Atiyeh*] (end note, Alfoneh, The Revolutionary Guards' Looting of Iran's Economy, p8)

Appendix 4[109]

Companies Entirely or Partially Owned by
Mehr-e Eghtesad-e Iranian Investment Company
Azerbaijan Development Investment Company [*Sarmayehgozari-ye Tose'eh-ye Azerbaijan*]
Iran Aluminum Company [*Sherkat-e Alouminium-e Iran*]
Iran Marine Industrial Company [*Sherkat-e San'ati-ye Daryayi-ye Iran*]
Iran Mineral Products Company [*Sherkat-e Faravari-ye Mavad-e Ma'dani-ye Iran*]
Iran Industrial Development [*Tose'eh-ye San'ati-ye Iran*]
Iran Tractor Factory [*Traktorsazi-ye Iran*]
Iran Tractor Foundry Company [*Rikhtegariye Traktorsazi-ye Iran*]
Iran Zinc Mines Development Company [*Tose'eh-ye Ma'aden-e Rouy*]
Isfahan Mobarakeh Steelwork [*Foulad-e Mobarakeh-ye Esfahan*]
Jaber Ben Hayan Pharmaceuticals [*Darousazi-ye Jaber Ben Hayan*]
Middle East Tidewater Company [*Tidewater-e Khavar-e Mianeh*]
Parsian Bank [*Bank-e Parsian*]
Sadid Pipe and Equipment Company [*Sherkat-e Louleh Va Tajhizat-e Sadid*]
Tabriz Tractor Factory [*Traktorsazi-ye Tabriz*]
Technotar Engineering Company [*Sherkat-e Mohandesi-ye Teknotar*]
Tous-Gostar Investment Company [*Sarmayehgozari-ye Tous-Gostar*] (end note, Alfoneh, The Revolutionary Guards' Looting of Iran's Economy, p8)

Main Subsidiaries of the Basij Cooperative Foundation
Basij Housing Foundation [*Moassesseh-ye Ta'min-e Maskan-e Basij*]
No-Interest Loan Institute of the Basij Members [*Moassesseh-ye Gharz al-Hassaneh-ye Basijian*]
Consumer-Goods Provision Foundation of the Basij Members [*Moassesseh-ye Ta'min-e Aghlam-e Masrafi-ye Basijian*]
Cultural/Artistic Institute of the Warriors of Islam [*Moassesseh-ye Farhangi/Honari-ye Razmandegan-e Eslam*]
Scientific and Pedagogic Services Institute of the Basij Members [*Moassesseh-ye Khadamat-e Elmi Va Amouzeshi-ye Razmandegan*]

Table 1: Exploitation Options

Instrument of National Power	Exploitable Vulnerability	WOGs Exploitation Options (current)
Diplomatic	- Inconsistency with Khomeini's guidance	- Expose IRGC involvement and interference in politics
	- Reliance on SL Khamenei	- Expose IRGC dismissal of executive, judicial, and legislative branches' authority
	- State sponsorship of terrorism	- Increase scope and breadth of sanctions, convince Islamic nations to declare Iran a state sponsor of terrorism
	- Expediency principle over tenets of Islam	- Enlist support of other Islamic nations (Turkey, GCC, Pakistan) to demarche Iran for violations of tenets of Islam
	- Opposition of Quietist clerics	- Enlist support of other Islamic nations to support and reinforce Quietist position
	- Factionalism among IRGC officers and alumni	- Establish dialogue with moderate and pragmatic IRGC leaders
	- Displacement of trained diplomats	- Expose IRGC officers operating under diplomatic cover and expel them from embassies and consulates
Informational	- Inherent contradictions in indoctrination	- Expose and illuminate the contradictions, encourage dissent and free thought and speech, denounce human rights violations and oppression
	- inability to block electronic media	- Promote and proliferate technology, provide cyber infrastructure for free flow of information
	- oppression of journalists	- Impose additional sanctions for violations of human rights, provide journalists avenues for disseminating reports
	- reliance on cyber terrorism	- retaliate proportionally to cyber attacks against individuals, organizations, and cyber infrastructure; sanction individuals and organizations responsible for attacks
Military	- Violating constitutionally	- Declare the IRGC and Basij hostile terrorist entities without the protections

	mandated C2	normally afforded military services under the Geneva Conventions and LOAC.
	- Duality of IRGC and *Artesh*	- Establish dialogue with senior Artesh leadership, guarantee conditional protection in the event of conflict
	- Flawed doctrine	- Indict IRGC leadership for sponsoring terrorism; seize all IRGC and IRGC affiliated financial assets; encourage Basij to refute martyrdom operations; retaliate proportionally against IRGC sponsored terrorists; employ information operations aggressively and proactively to discredit IRGC propaganda
	- Historical revisionism	- Provide accurate historical reports on IRGC policy and strategy that cost Iran thousands of lives
Economic	- Intentional economic isolation	- Extend sanctions to all IRGC and state owned banking and financial institutions, indict individuals and corporations violating sanctions and seize their assets
	- Extralegal activity in Black and Gray Market	- Support border control efforts by Iran's neighbors; designate IRGC owned ports, jetties, and transportation services as material supporters of terrorism and seize their assets; expose IRGC leaders' illegal accumulation of wealth
	- Destruction of merchant class	- Expose the fallacy of Iranian economic privatization; expose all foundations, businesses, and cooperatives that are IRGC owned or affiliated and seize their assets
	- Ineptitude in running the economy	- Continue to block IMF and World Bank support to Iran due to lack of transparency in economic planning, banking, and finance
	- shrinking export markets	- Aggressively support alternative oil and gas sources for India, China and Japan; support direct foreign investment in gas

	- Inconsistent messaging ref sanctions	pipelines that reduce reliance on Iranian natural gas - Expose the opportunity cost the IRGC has imposed on the Iranian economy through its flawed military strategy and its self serving management of the economy

Endnotes

[1] *Constitution of the Islamic Republic of Iran*, chap. IX, article 150, http://www.iranchamber.com/government/laws/constitution_ch09.php (accessed AUG 24, 2011).

[2] Frederick Wehrey, *Rise of the Pasdaran. Assessing the Domestic Roles of Iran's Islamic Revolutionary Guard Corps,* (Santa Monica, CA, RAND Corporation, 2009), 21.

[3] Kenneth Katzman, Iran: U.S. Concerns and Policy Responses, (Washington, DC: U.S. Library of Congress, Congressional Research Service, April 18, 2011), 24.

[4] Ash Jane, "Nuclear Weapons and Iran's Global Ambitions: Troubling Scenarios," *Washington Institute for Near East Policy*, no. 114, (August 2011), 25.

[5] Jahangir Arasli, "Obsolete Weapons, Unconventional Tactics, and Martyrdom Zeal: How Iran Would Apply its Asymmetric Naval Warfare doctrine in a Future Conflict," *George C. Marshall European Center for Security Studies Occasional Paper Series,* no. 10, (April 2007): 44.

[6] *Jane's Sentinel Security Assessment - The Gulf States, Iran, 05 AUG 2011,* http://www4.janes.com/subscribe/sentinel/GULFS_doc_view.jsp?Sent_Country=Iran&Prod_Name=GULFS&K2DocKey=/content1/janesdata/sent/gulfsu/irans010.htm@current, (accessed September 12, 2011).

[7] Ali Alfoneh, "What do Structural changes in the Revolutionary Guards Mean," *American Enterprise Institute Middle East Outlook*, (April 10, 2009).

[8] Ibid.

[9] Ibid.

[10] Jahangir Arasli, "Obsolete Weapons, Unconventional Tactics, and Martyrdom Zeal: How Iran Would Apply its Asymmetric Naval Warfare doctrine in a Future Conflict," *George C. Marshall European Center for Security Studies Occasional Paper Series,* no. 10, (April 2007): 11-12.

[11] Ibid, 12-13.

[12] Ibid, 40.

[13] Frederick Wehrey, *Rise of the Pasdaran. Assessing the Domestic Roles of Iran's Islamic Revolutionary Guard Corps,* (Santa Monica, CA, RAND Corporation, 2009), 2.

[14] *Jane's Sentinel Security Assessment - The Gulf States, Iran, 05 AUG 2011,* http://www4.janes.com/subscribe/sentinel/GULFS_doc_view.jsp?Sent_Country=Iran&Prod_Name=GULFS&K2DocKey=/content1/janesdata/sent/gulfsu/irans010.htm@current, (accessed September 12, 2011).

[15] Michael Eisenstadt, *The Strategic Culture of the Islamic Republic of Iran Operational and Policy Implications,* Middle East Studies at the Marine Corps University, MES Monographs , no. 1, (August 2011), 7.

[16] Mustafa Al-Sawwaf, "Iran Failed to 'Blackmail' HAMAS, 'Buy Political Positions' for Aid," *Gaza Filastin (Electronic Edition)* in Arabic, September 8, 2011, https://www.opensource.gov/portal/server.pt/gateway/PTARGS_0_0_200_307_521_43/content/Display/GMP20110908751001, (accessed September 9, 2011).

[17] Frederick Wehrey, *Rise of the Pasdaran. Assessing the Domestic Roles of Iran's Islamic Revolutionary Guard Corps,* (Santa Monica, CA, RAND Corporation, 2009), 43.

[18] Ibid, 83.

[19] Michael Eisenstadt, *The Strategic Culture of the Islamic Republic of Iran Operational and Policy Implications,* Middle East Studies at the Marine Corps University, MES Monographs , no. 1, (August 2011), 11.

[20] Jahangir Arasli, "Obsolete Weapons, Unconventional Tactics, and Martyrdom Zeal: How Iran Would Apply its Asymmetric Naval Warfare doctrine in a Future Conflict," *George C. Marshall European Center for Security Studies Occasional Paper Series,* no. 10, (April 2007): 41.

[21] `Angus Stickler and Maggie O'Kane, "Former Elite Officers Reveal Tensions in Iran Regime," June 11, 2010, *Guardian Films, Bureau of Investigative Journalism*, video file, http://www.guardian.co.uk/world/2010/jun/11/iran-revolutionary-guards-regime, (accessed September 15, 2011).

[22] Ibid

[23] Frederick Wehrey, *Rise of the Pasdaran. Assessing the Domestic Roles of Iran's Islamic Revolutionary Guard Corps,* (Santa Monica, CA, RAND Corporation, 2009), 78.

[24] Ed Blanche, "Pasdaran Power," The Middle East, no. 360, (October 2005), 22-23.

[25] Afshon P. Ostovar, "Guardians of the Islamic Revolution: Ideology, Politics, and the Development of Military Power in Iran," A dissertation submitted in partial fulfillment

of the requirements for the degree of Doctor of Philosophy (History) in The University of Michigan, 2009, http://proquest.umi.com/pqdweb?index=0&did=1963690761&SrchMode=2&sid=1&Fmt=

6&VInst=PROD&VType=PQD&RQT=309&VName=PQD&TS=1315305979&clientId=111 53, (accessed 6 Sept 2011), 173.

[26]Ed Blanche, "Pasdaran Power," The Middle East, no. 360, (October 2005), 22-24.

[27] Stephen Kaufman, "Iranian Decisions Increasingly Being Made by Revolutionary Guard," America.gov, February 17, 2010, available at http://www.america.gov/st/peacesec-english/2010/February/20100217145832esnamfuak0.6569178.html (accessed 6 Sept, 2011).

[28] *Constitution of the Islamic Republic of Iran*, chap. IX, article 150, http://www.iranchamber.com/government/laws/constitution_ch09.php (accessed AUG 24, 2011).

[29] "Khatam ol-Anbia Will Not Compete With Private Sector," Tehran *Jam-e Jam Online* in Persian, August 8, 2011, https://www.opensource.gov/portal/server.pt/gateway/PTARGS_0_0_2348_307_521_43/content/Display/PRINCE/IAP20110808513005

(accessed August 29, 2011).

[30] "Commander Ja'fari on IRGC's Economic Activities," Tehran *Siyasat-e Ruz Online* in Persian, August 8, 2011, https://www.opensource.gov/portal/server.pt/gateway/PTARGS_0_0_2348_307_521_43/content/Display/PRINCE/IAP20110808513008, (accessed August 29, 2011).

[31] "Deputy IRGC Chief: Our War Is In Defense Of Our Land, Beliefs, And Identity,"

Tehran *IRNA* in English, August 8, 2011, https://www.opensource.gov/portal/server.pt/gateway/PTARGS_0_0_2348_307_521_43/content/Display/PRINCE/IAP20110808950120, (Accessed August 29, 2011).

[32] *Constitution of the Islamic Republic of Iran*, chap. IX, article 150, http://www.iranchamber.com/government/laws/constitution_ch09.php (accessed AUG 24, 2011).

[33] Frederick Wehrey, *Rise of the Pasdaran. Assessing the Domestic Roles of Iran's Islamic Revolutionary Guard Corps,* (Santa Monica, CA, RAND Corporation, 2009), 78.

[33] Ed Blanche, "Pasdaran Power," The Middle East, no. 360, (October 2005), 83.

[34] Angus Stickler and Maggie O'Kane, "Former Elite Officers Reveal Tensions in Iran Regime," June 11, 2010, *Guardian Films, Bureau of Investigative Journalism*, video file, http://www.guardian.co.uk/world/2010/jun/11/iran-revolutionary-guards-regime, (accessed September 15, 2011).

[35] Afshon P. Ostovar, "Guardians of the Islamic Revolution: Ideology, Politics, and the Development of Military Power in Iran," A dissertation submitted in partial fulfillment of the requirements for the degree of Doctor of Philosophy (History) in The University of

Michigan, 2009,
http://proquest.umi.com/pqdweb?index=0&did=1963690761&SrchMode=2&sid=1&Fmt=
6&VInst=PROD&VType=PQD&RQT=309&VName=PQD&TS=1315305979&clientId=111
53, (accessed 6 Sept 2011), 169-171.

[36] Kenneth Katzman, Iran: U.S. Concerns and Policy Responses, (Washington, DC:
U.S. Library of Congress, Congressional Research Service, April 18, 2011), 9-11.

[37] US Department of State Country Reports on Terrorism 2010, August 18, 2011,
Chapters 3 and 6, http://www.state.gov/s/ct/rls/crt/2010/170260.htm, (accessed August
24, 2011).

[38] "European Union Council Implementing Regulation (EU) No 611/2011

of 23 June 2011, implementing Regulation (EU) No 442/2011 concerning restrictive
measures in view of the situation in Syria," http://eur-
lex.europa.eu/LexUriServ/LexUriServ.do?uri=OJ:L:2011:164:0001:0003:EN:PDF,
(accessed 30 AUG).

[39] "Administration Takes Additional Steps to Hold the Government of Syria
Accountable for Violent Repression Against the Syrian People," US Department of
Treasury Press Center, May 18, 2011, http://www.treasury.gov/press-center/press-
releases/Pages/tg1181.aspx (accessed August 30, 2011).

[40] Frederick Wehrey, Rise of the Pasdaran. Assessing the Domestic Roles of Iran's
Islamic Revolutionary Guard Corps, (Santa Monica, CA, RAND Corporation, 2009), 79-
80.

[41] Michael Eisenstadt, The Strategic Culture of the Islamic Republic of Iran
Operational and Policy Implications, Middle East Studies at the Marine Corps University,
MES Monographs , no. 1, (August 2011), 2-3.

[42] Angus Stickler and Maggie O'Kane, "Former Elite Officers Reveal Tensions in
Iran Regime," June 11, 2010, Guardian Films, Bureau of Investigative Journalism, video
file, http://www.guardian.co.uk/world/2010/jun/11/iran-revolutionary-guards-regime,
(accessed September 15, 2011).

[43] Kenneth Katzman, Iran: U.S. Concerns and Policy Responses, (Washington, DC:
U.S. Library of Congress, Congressional Research Service, April 18, 2011), 4-5.

[44] Ali Alfoneh, "All Ahmadinejad's Men," Middle East Quarterly, (Spring 2011), 79-84.

[45] "Iran: Article Assesses Development of Political Guide Corps for Basij, IRGC,"

Tehran Fars News Agency in Persian, August 3, 2011,
https://www.opensource.gov/portal/server.pt/gateway/PTARGS_0_0_2348_307_521_43
/content/Display/PRINCE/IAP20110803690001, (accessed August 29, 2011).

[46] Ali Alfoneh, "Indoctrination of the Revolutionary Guards," American Enterprise
Institute Middle East Outlook, (February 20, 2009),

http://www.irantracker.org/analysis/indoctrination-revolutionary-guards (accessed 31 AUG 11).

[47] Afshon P. Ostovar, "Guardians of the Islamic Revolution: Ideology, Politics, and the Development of Military Power in Iran," A dissertation submitted in partial fulfillment

of the requirements for the degree of Doctor of Philosophy (History) in The University of Michigan, 2009, http://proquest.umi.com/pqdweb?index=0&did=1963690761&SrchMode=2&sid=1&Fmt=6&VInst=PROD&VType=PQD&RQT=309&VName=PQD&TS=1315305979&clientId=11153, (accessed 6 Sept 2011), 186.

[48] Frederick Wehrey, *Rise of the Pasdaran. Assessing the Domestic Roles of Iran's Islamic Revolutionary Guard Corps,* (Santa Monica, CA, RAND Corporation, 2009), 35-49.

[49] Ali Alfoneh, "Indoctrination of the Revolutionary Guards," *American Enterprise Institute Middle East Outlook*, (February 20, 2009), http://www.irantracker.org/analysis/indoctrination-revolutionary-guards (accessed 31 AUG 11).

[50] "Iran -- Overview of Security Services' Virtual Presence," Open Source Center Report, May 20, 2011,

https://www.opensource.gov/portal/server.pt/gateway/PTARGS_0_0_828_307_0_43/content/Display/GMP20110520431002 (accessed September 13, 2011).

[51] Ibid.

[52] "Iran To Launch National E-Mail Service," *Mardomak* in Persian, September 8, 2011, https://www.opensource.gov/portal/server.pt/gateway/PTARGS_0_0_200_307_521_43/content/Display/IAP20110908950017, (accessed September 8, 2011).

[53] Saeed Kamali Deghan, "Iran Newspaper Closed Down Amid Row Over Mahmoud Ahmadinejad Satire," guardian.co.uk, September 6, 2011, http://www.guardian.co.uk/world/2011/sep/06/iran-newspaper-closed-ahmadinejad-satire (accessed September 7, 2011).

[54] "Iranian Net Users Hacked After Security Breach in Holland," *Reuters, guardian.co.uk*, September 6, 2011,

http://www.guardian.co.uk/technology/2011/sep/06/hacker-iran-holland-certificates, (accessed September 7, 2011).

[55] Charles Arthur, "DigiNotar SSL Certificate Hack Amounts to Cyberwar, Says Expert," *guardian.co.uk*, September 5, 2011, http://www.guardian.co.uk/technology/2011/sep/05/diginotar-certificate-hack-cyberwar?INTCMP=ILCNETTXT3487, (accessed September 7, 2011).

[56] Richard A. Clarke, Robert K. Knake, "Securing the GCC in Cyberspace," *Emirates Center for Strategic Studies and Research*, *Emirates Lecture Series*, issue 83, 2010, http://proquest.umi.com/pqdweb?index=2&did=2331073461&SrchMode=2&sid=1&Fmt=3&VInst=PROD&VType=PQD&RQT=309&VName=PQD&TS=1316168915&clientId=111 53, (accessed September 15, 2011).

[57] "'Cyber Hezbollah' Begins Activities Online," *Ya Lesarat ol-Hoseyn,* Tehran, September 1, 2011, https://www.opensource.gov/portal/server.pt/gateway/PTARGS_0_0_200_203_121123_43/content/Display/IAP20110901397005#index=4&searchKey=6049660&rpp=10, (accessed September 8, 2011).

[58] "BBCM Profile: Iran's 'Cyber Hezbollah' Network," Open Source Center Feature, *BBC Monitoring*, September 26, 2001, https://www.opensource.gov/portal/server.pt/gateway/PTARGS_0_0_2350_307_521_43/content/Display/24715557, (accessed September 27, 2001).

[59] "Fars Reports Official's Remarks About Iranians' Use of 'Immoral Sites'," *Tehran Fars News Agency*, August 26, 2011, https://www.opensource.gov/portal/server.pt/gateway/PTARGS_0_0_200_203_121123_43/content/Display/IAP20110829950107#index=6&searchKey=6049660&rpp=10 (accessed September 8, 2011).

[60] Frederick Wehrey, *Rise of the Pasdaran. Assessing the Domestic Roles of Iran's Islamic Revolutionary Guard Corps,* (Santa Monica, CA, RAND Corporation, 2009), 50-51.

[61] Ali Alfoneh, "Indoctrination of the Revolutionary Guards," *American Enterprise Institute Middle East Outlook*, (February 20, 2009), http://www.irantracker.org/analysis/indoctrination-revolutionary-guards (accessed 31 AUG 11).

[62] Julie Tomlin, "Social media gives women a voice in Iran," guardian.co.uk, september 22, 2011, http://www.guardian.co.uk/lifeandstyle/2011/sep/22/social-media-women-iran, (accessed September 26, 2011).

[63] Angus Stickler and Maggie O'Kane, "Former Elite Officers Reveal Tensions in Iran Regime," June 11, 2010, *Guardian Films, Bureau of Investigative Journalism*, video file, http://www.guardian.co.uk/world/2010/jun/11/iran-revolutionary-guards-regime, (accessed September 15, 2011).

[64] Richard A. Clarke, Robert K. Knake, "Securing the GCC in Cyberspace," *Emirates Center for Strategic Studies and Research*, *Emirates Lecture Series*, issue 83, 2010, http://proquest.umi.com/pqdweb?index=2&did=2331073461&SrchMode=2&sid=1&Fmt=3&VInst=PROD&VType=PQD&RQT=309&VName=PQD&TS=1316168915&clientId=111 53, (accessed September 15, 2011).

[65] "Commander Ja'fari on IRGC's Economic Activities," *Siyasat-e Ruze Online*, Tehran, August 8, 2011,

https://www.opensource.gov/portal/server.pt/gateway/PTARGS_0_0_2348_307_521_43/content/Display/PRINCE/IAP20110808513008, (Accessed August 29, 2011)

[66] "IRGC: Khatam ol-Anbia Will Not Compete With Private Sector," Jam-e Jam Online, Tehran, August 8, 2011, https://www.opensource.gov/portal/server.pt/gateway/PTARGS_0_0_2348_307_521_43/content/Display/PRINCE/IAP20110808513005, (accessed August 29, 2011).

[67] *Constitution of the Islamic Republic of Iran*, chap. IX, article 150, http://www.iranchamber.com/government/laws/constitution_ch09.php (accessed August 24, 2011).

[68] *Constitution of the Islamic Republic of Iran*, chap. IV, art. 44, available at http://www.iranchamber.com/government/laws/constitution_ch04.php (accessed August 24, 2011).

[69] Kenneth Katzman, Iran: U.S. Concerns and Policy Responses, (Washington, DC: U.S. Library of Congress, Congressional Research Service, April 18, 2011), 24.

[70] Ali Alfoneh, "The Revolutionary Guards Looting of Iran's Economy," *American Enterprise Institute Middle East Outlook*, no. 3, (June, 2010), http://www.aei.org/outlook/100969 (accessed September 16, 2011)

[71] Ibid.

[72] "Country Report, Iran," *Economist Intelligence Unit*, London, August, 2011, 3.

[73] Ali Alfoneh, "The Revolutionary Guards Looting of Iran's Economy," *American Enterprise Institute Middle East Outlook*, no. 3, (June, 2010), http://www.aei.org/outlook/100969 (accessed September 16, 2011)

[74] Saeed Kamali Dehghan, "Iran Revolutionary Guards' Commander Set to Become President of OPEC," *guardian.co.uk*, July 27, 2011, http://www.guardian.co.uk/world/2011/jul/27/iran-revolutionary-guards-opec-rostam-ghasemi?INTCMP=SRCH#history-link-box, (accessed August 2, 2011).

[75] *Jane's Sentinel Security Assessment - The Gulf States, Iran, 05 AUG 2011*, http://www4.janes.com/subscribe/sentinel/GULFS_doc_view.jsp?Sent_Country=Iran&Prod_Name=GULFS&K2DocKey=/content1/janesdata/sent/gulfsu/irans010.htm@current, (accessed September 12, 2011).

[76] Frederick Wehrey, *Rise of the Pasdaran. Assessing the Domestic Roles of Iran's Islamic Revolutionary Guard Corps*, (Santa Monica, CA, RAND Corporation, 2009), 57-59.

[77] Elliot Hen-Tov, "Understanding Iran's New Authoritarianism," *Washington Quarterly*, 30, no. 1 (Winter 2006-2007): 174.

[78] Frederick Wehrey, *Rise of the Pasdaran. Assessing the Domestic Roles of Iran's Islamic Revolutionary Guard Corps,* (Santa Monica, CA, RAND Corporation, 2009), 65-66.

[79] *Jane's Sentinel Security Assessment - The Gulf States, Iran, 05 AUG 2011,* http://www4.janes.com/subscribe/sentinel/GULFS_doc_view.jsp?Sent_Country=Iran&Prod_Name=GULFS&K2DocKey=/content1/janesdata/sent/gulfsu/irans010.htm@current, (accessed September 12, 2011).

[80] "IRGC: Khatam ol-Anbia Will Not Compete With Private Sector," Jam-e Jam Online, Tehran, August 8, 2011, https://www.opensource.gov/portal/server.pt/gateway/PTARGS_0_0_2348_307_521_43/content/Display/PRINCE/IAP20110808513005, (accessed August 29, 2011).

[81] "Country Report, Iran," *Economist Intelligence Unit*, London, August, 2011, 15.

[82] "Analysis: Indian Debt Row Suggests Sanctions Stress Iran," *Open Source Center Analysis*, September 12 2011, https://www.opensource.gov/portal/server.pt/gateway/PTARGS_0_0_2348_307_521_43/content/Display/24604120, (accessed September 16, 2011).

[83] Frederick Wehrey, *Rise of the Pasdaran. Assessing the Domestic Roles of Iran's Islamic Revolutionary Guard Corps,* (Santa Monica, CA, RAND Corporation, 2009), 64.

[84] Ibid, 64.

[85] Ibid, 73-74.

[86] Ali Alfoneh, "Iran's Secret Network: Major General Qassem Suleimani's Inner Circle," *American Enterprise Institute Middle East Outlook*, no. 2, (March 2011), 1.

[87] Kenneth Katzman, Iran: U.S. Concerns and Policy Responses, (Washington, DC: U.S. Library of Congress, Congressional Research Service, April 18, 2011), 24.

[88] Ali Alfoneh, "Iran's Secret Network: Major General Qassem Suleimani's Inner Circle," *American Enterprise Institute Middle East Outlook*, no. 2, (March 2011), 3-4.

[89] Afshon P. Ostovar, "Guardians of the Islamic Revolution: Ideology, Politics, and the Development of Military Power in Iran," A dissertation submitted in partial fulfillment

of the requirements for the degree of Doctor of Philosophy (History) in The University of Michigan, 2009, http://proquest.umi.com/pqdweb?index=0&did=1963690761&SrchMode=2&sid=1&Fmt=6&VInst=PROD&VType=PQD&RQT=309&VName=PQD&TS=1315305979&clientId=11153, (accessed 6 Sept 2011), 118-120.

[90] "CENTCOM in 2010: Views from General David H. Petraeus," *Institute for the Study of War*, www.understandingwar.org/press-media/webcast/centcom-2010-views-general-david-h-petraeus-video, (accessed August 20, 2011).

[91] Martin Chulov, "Qassem Suleimani: The Iranian General 'Secretly Running' Iraq," *guardian.co.uk*, 28 July, 2011, http://www.guardian.co.uk/world/2011/jul/28/qassem-suleimani-iran-iraq-influence, (accessed 20AUG 2011).

[92] Ibid.

[93] Ibid.

[94] Maseh Zarif, "Iran's Strategic Offensive in Iraq," *American Enterprise Institute, Iran Tracker,* July 2011, http://www.irantracker.org/analysis/irans-strategic-offensive-iraq, (accessed September 16, 2011).

[95] Kenneth Katzman, Iran: U.S. Concerns and Policy Responses, (Washington, DC: U.S. Library of Congress, Congressional Research Service, April 18, 2011), 44-45.

[96] Ibid, 44-45.

[97] Ali Alfoneh, "Iran's Most Dangerous General," *American Enterprise Institute Middle East Outlook*, no. 4, (July 2011), 1.

[98] Michael H. Posner, Jeffrey D. Feltman, "U.S. Human Rights Policy toward Iran and Syria," *Statement Before the House Foreign Affairs Committee, Subcommittee on the Middle East and South Asia,* (July 27, 2011), http://www.state.gov/g/drl/rls/rm/2011/169180.htm, (accessed August 30, 2011).

[99] Hillary Clinton, *US Department of State Country reports on Terrorism 2010*, (Washington, DC: U.S. Department of State, August, 2011), http://www.state.gov/s/ct/rls/crt/2010/170260.htm, (accessed August 24, 2011).

[100] "Administration Takes Additional Steps to Hold the Government of Syria Accountable for Violent Repression Against the Syrian People," *US Department of Treasury Press Center*, May 5, 2011, http://www.treasury.gov/press-center/press-releases/Pages/tg1181.aspx, (accessed August 30, 2011).

[101] Martin Chulov, "Qassem Suleimani: The Iranian General 'Secretly Running' Iraq," *guardian.co.uk*, 28 July, 2011, http://www.guardian.co.uk/world/2011/jul/28/qassem-suleimani-iran-iraq-influence, (accessed 20AUG 2011).

[102] Stephen Kaufman, "Iranian Decisions Increasingly Being Made by Revolutionary Guard," America.gov, February 17, 2010, available at http://www.america.gov/st/peacesec-english/2010/February/20100217145832esnamfuak0.6569178.html (accessed 6 Sept, 2011).

[103] Barak H. Obama, *The National Security Strategy of the United States of America* (Washington, DC: The White House, May 2010), 7.

[104] Frederick Wehrey, *Rise of the Pasdaran. Assessing the Domestic Roles of Iran's Islamic Revolutionary Guard Corps,* (Santa Monica, CA, RAND Corporation, 2009), 103-107.

[105] Ali Alfoneh, "All Ahmadinejad's Men", *Middle East Quarterly*, (Spring 2011), http://www.meforum.org/2935/ahmadinejad-power-struggle (accessed September 21, 2011).

[106] "Iranian Biographies and Photos ," *Wikis on OpenSource.gov,* https://www.opensource.gov/wiki/display/IranianBios/B+-+Iranian+Biographies+and+Photos, (accessed September 21, 2011).

[107] Ali Alfoneh, "The Revolutionary Guards Looting of Iran's Economy," *American Enterprise Institute Middle East Outlook*, no. 3, (June, 2010), http://www.aei.org/outlook/100969 (accessed September 16, 2011).

[108] Ibid.

[109] Ibid.

[110] Ibid.